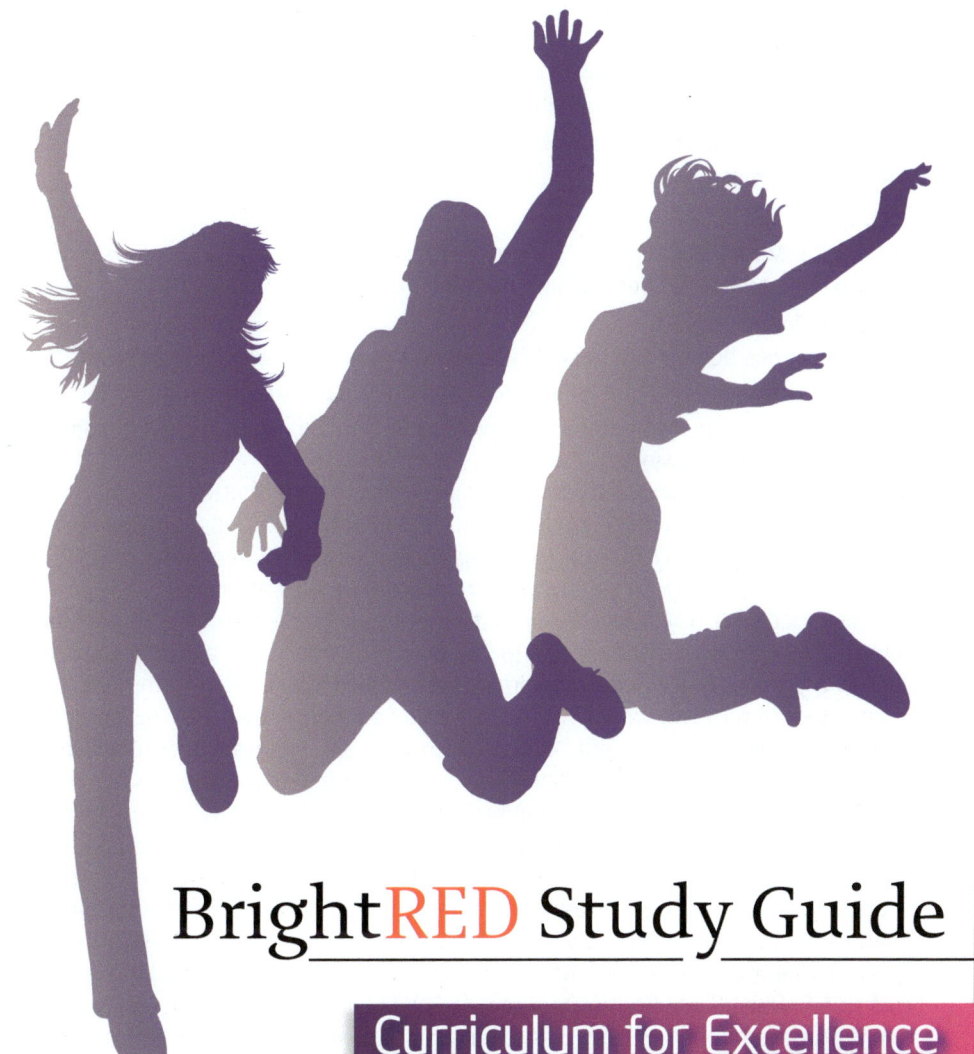

BrightRED Study Guide

Curriculum for Excellence

N5

MEDIA

Alexandra Mattinson

First published in 2020 by:
Bright Red Publishing Ltd
1 Torphichen Street
Edinburgh
EH3 8HX

Copyright © Bright Red Publishing Ltd 2020

Cover image © Caleb Rutherford

All rights reserved. No part of this publication may be reproduced, stored in a retrieval system, or transmitted in any form or by any means, electronic, mechanical, photocopying, recording or otherwise, without prior permission in writing from the publisher.

The rights of Alexandra Mattinson to be identified as the author of this work have been asserted by them in accordance with Sections 77 and 78 of the Copyright, Designs and Patents Act 1988.

A CIP record for this book is available from the British Library.

ISBN 978-1-84948-307-0

With thanks to:
PDQ Digital Media Solutions Ltd, Bungay (layout), Lauren Booth (copy-edit).
Cover design and series book design by Caleb Rutherford – e i d e t i c.

Acknowledgements
Every effort has been made to seek all copyright-holders. If any have been overlooked, then Bright Red Publishing will be delighted to make the necessary arrangements.

Permission has been sought from all relevant copyright holders and Bright Red Publishing are grateful for the use of the following:

Rawpixel.com/Shutterstock.com (p 4); Alexander Supertramp/Shutterstock.com (p 4); Sergey Nivens/Shutterstock.com (p 5); MSSA/Shutterstock.com (p 8); MaxterDesign/Shutterstock.com (p 8); Forsaken Fotos (CC BY 2.0)[4] (p 10); anthony kelly (CC BY 2.0)[4] (p 10); tableatny (CC BY 2.0)[4] (p 11); Poprugin Aleksey/Shutterstock.com (p 17); Alain LEONARD/Creative Commons (CC BY-SA 2.0)[1] (p 17); geen graphy/Shutterstock.com (p 18); Two images by JoyImage/Shutterstock.com (p 19); Phovoir/Shutterstock.com (p 19); Macrovector/Shutterstock.com (p 19); bleakstar/Shutterstock.com (p 20); hidesy/Shutterstock.com (p 21); aga7ta/Shutterstock.com (p 22); Boris15/Shutterstock.com (p 24); Loren Javier/Creative Commons (CC BY-ND 2.0)[2] (p 24); Image(s licensed by Ingram Image (p 26); Ji-Elle/Creative Commons (CC BY-SA 3.0)[3] (p 26); Everett Historical/Shutterstock.com (p 28); Woody Hibbard/Creative Commons (CC BY 2.0)[4] (p 32); sergio barbieri/Creative Commons (CC BY-SA 2.0)[1] (p 32); Lutsenko_Oleksandr/Shutterstock.com (p 33); Images Money/Creative Commons (CC BY 2.0)[4] (p 33); Ollyy/Shutterstock.com (p 35); Insanet/Shutterstock.com (p 35); JozephT/Shutterstock.com (p 35); puuikibeach/Creative Commons (CC BY 2.0)[4] (p 36); Rawpixel.com/Shutterstock.com (p 38); qvist/Shutterstock.com (p 38); chrisdorney/Shutterstock.com (p 38); Hadrian/Shutterstock.com (p 39); Lenscap Photography/Shutterstock.com (p 39); Hadrian/Shutterstock.com (p 40); Timofeev Vladimir/Shutterstock.com (p 41); Markus Grossalber/Creative Commons (CC BY 2.0)[4] (p 44); Haywiremedia/Shutterstock.com (p 48); Oliver Denker/Shutterstock.com (p 49); Everett Historical/Shutterstock.com (p 50); aderi/Shutterstock.com (p 50); Nicholas A. Tonelli/Creative Commons (CC BY 2.0)[4] (p 51); uselessid/Creative Commons (CC BY 2.0)[4] (p 51); kristarella/Creative Commons (CC BY-SA 2.0)1 (p 52); Trueffelpix/Shutterstock.com (p 52); Arthimedes/Shutterstock.com (p 53); Hurst Photo/Shutterstock.com (p 53); Monkey Business Images/Shutterstock.com (p 53); Andrey_Popov/Shutterstock.com (p 53); Factory_Easy/Shutterstock.com (p 53); ShutterOK/Shutterstock.com (p 53); Stokkete/Shutterstock.com (p 53); Rawpixel.com/Shutterstock.com (p 54); NME magazine cover from 30 July 2011 featuring Amy Winehouse © Dean Chalkley (p 55); claudia veja images/Shutterstock.com (p 55); Africa Studio/Shutterstock.com (p 56); Gary Campbell-Hall/Creative Commons (CC BY 2.0)[4] (p 56); Jirsak/Shutterstock.com (p 57); Natee Photo/Shutterstock.com (p 58); Hilch/Shutterstock.com (p 59); Ayrshire Magazine cover (No 18 – Sept/Oct 2017) is reproduced with permission of Ayrshire Magazine (p 61); Jeep advert from the Renegade Campaign by Gitanos, July 2017, is reproduced by permission of FCA Group (p 61); Mini advert by Chemistry, October 2013, is reproduced by permission of BMW Group (p 63); MOJO magazine cover (July 2009) is reproduced by permission of Bauer Consumer Media Ltd (p 64); Nungning20/Shutterstock.com (p 66); Lindebornt/Creative Commons (CC BY-ND 2.0)[2] (p 68); David Michalczuk/Creative Commons (CC BY 2.0)[4] (p 68); Bernard Goldbach/Creative Commons (CC BY 2.0)[4] (p 68); SkyLynx/Shutterstock.com (p 70); Mark Poprocki/Shutterstock.com (p 71); Korawat photo shoot/Shutterstock.com (p 72); Tomacco/Shutterstock.com (p 72); NikWB/Shutterstock.com (pp 73 & 74); Rawpixel.com/Shutterstock.com (p 74); Lorelyn Medina/Shutterstock.com (p 76); Raywoo/Shutterstock.com (p 76); Rawpixel.com/Shutterstock.com (p 84); Shayli/Shutterstock.com (p 85); GaudiLab/Shutterstock.com (p 85); Twinsterphoto/Shutterstock.com (p 86); Text from YouTube: https://support.google.com/youtube/answer/2802008?hl=en-GB © Google (p 86); PixieMe/Shutterstock.com (p 86); NineBrassMonkeys YouTube home page is reproduced by permission of Benjamin Cook (p 87); Robert Scoble/Creative Commons (CC BY 2.0)[4] (p 88); Featureflash Photo Agency/Shutterstock.com (p 90); Maslowski Marcin/Shutterstock.com (p 91); Oliver Denker/Shutterstock.com (p 94).

[1] (CC BY-SA 2.0) http://creativecommons.org/licenses/by-sa/2.0/
[2] (CC BY-ND 2.0) http://creativecommons.org/licenses/by-nd/2.0/
[3] (CC BY-SA 3.0) https://creativecommons.org/licenses/by-sa/3.0/
[4] (CC BY 2.0) http://creativecommons.org/licenses/by/2.0/

CONTENTS

INTRODUCING NATIONAL 5 MEDIA
1. The role of media.................................4
2. Course outline 6
3. Categories.......................................8

LANGUAGE
4. Camera work................................... 10
5. Editing 12
6. Sound... 14
7. Lighting 16
8. Print language 18
9. Persuasion and emotive language............. 20

REPRESENTATION
10. Ideologies...................................... 22
11. Stereotypes 24

NARRATIVE
12. Narrative 1 26
13. Narrative 2 28
14. Narrative 3 30

INSTITUTIONS
14. Internal constraints 32
15. External constraints........................... 34
16. Advertising regulations........................ 36

NEWS CONTENT AND THE ROLE OF THE MEDIA
17. Newspaper formats 38
18. Press ownership, circulation, regulation and fake news................................... 40
19. Meeting needs and achieving particular purposes . 42
20. Influencing attitudes and behaviours............. 44
21. Non-fiction films and public information films 46

SOCIETY
22. Reflecting time, place and events 48
23. Examples of society aspects in film texts 50

AUDIENCE
24. Target audience and audience research............ 52
25. Audience appeal, responses and needs 1.......... 54
26. Audience appeal, responses and needs 2.......... 56

COURSE ASSESSMENT
27. The exam question paper......................... 58
28. Analysing print texts 60
29. How to tackle unseen analysis.................... 62
30. How to tackle unseen analysis cont'd 64
31. How to tackle unseen analysis cont'd 66
32. The assignment 68
33. Assignment 1 – pre-production................... 70
34. Assignment 2 – production....................... 72
35. Assignment 3 – post-production...................74
36. Marking instructions and further practice 76
37. Further practice 78
38. Practice papers 80
39. Messages from the markers 82
40. How to research 84
41. Case study 1 – YouTube and vlogging............. 86
42. Case Study 2 – radio broadcasting................. 88
43. Case study 3 – radio content 90
44. Case study 4 – social realism 92
45. Case Study 5 – *Apocalypse Now* 94

GLOSSARY 96

INTRODUCING NATIONAL 5 MEDIA

THE ROLE OF MEDIA

WHAT IS MEANT BY MEDIA?

We live, work and play in a world saturated in and dependent upon multiple **forms** of media. It is quite simply central to our lives.

Media comes from the word '**medium**', which refers to the various channels that we use to communicate. 'Media' is the plural of medium (communication) and generally speaking relates to broadcast, print and online media.

What is media studies?

Media studies explores the impact of mass communication on society and this in turn affects how we make sense of our world. Throughout this guide you will learn to explore and analyse the seven key aspects of the course content. There are a range of theories and key ideas which will help you to explore both the impact of society on media and the impact on media from society.

Why it matters.

We live in a world where we are completely dependent on media. The connections between the news industry, ownership and politics are such that they heavily influence what information we are presented with. The power of advertising is such that it can convince us not only to buy into a product but to subscribe to a (potentially unrealistic) lifestyle. It forces us to judge and compare our own lives with an entirely fictional world; constructed by creators who are experts at identifying our fears, insecurities and greatest desires, and then selling us 'a solution' to get us one step closer to our dreams. Entertainment can act as a mirror, reflecting both an ugly and beautiful picture of the world in which we live. It can challenge our beliefs and values, provide an escape and meet our needs. It would be hard to imagine a modern world without, for example, social media. The media is an immense industry, providing employment both directly and indirectly. It is also fun to study!

Beyond the classroom

Many pupils leave school, having completed a media qualification, to pursue a career in the industry. This is a great time to be a media student, as in the last couple of years about 75 per cent of media graduates have gone straight into employment. This is probably both because the industry acts as a gateway to such a variety of opportunities and because there are so many transferable skills associated with the subject that you will be considered a valuable asset!

WHAT SKILLS WILL I LEARN THROUGH PARTICIPATION IN A MEDIA COURSE?

The combination of analysis and production will arm you with an array of useful transferable skills.

Literacy is central to our success in learning. Media literacy requires that you become an expert in communication. Your skills in this area will become highly developed and, if you put in the effort, will give your CV the edge over many others.

Research – both the National 5 and Higher courses involve a considerable amount of research, most notably the planning section of your assignment. However, you will be researching new content and theories all the way through your course.

contd

Problem solving and creativity. In your assignment you will be required to negotiate a 'brief' and work through a number of institutional and creative problems. You will have to make, justify and evaluate planning decisions based on your research. With a low (or no) budget you will have to stretch your imagination to the limit by coming up with creative solutions (see the Assignment section) to ensure your product is finished to a high standard.

Working with others and leadership. You will need to communicate your plans clearly and concisely to others and learn to give clear and realistic instructions and deadlines. You will have to keep your cool (even if those around you don't) and show others in your group that you are reliable and responsible.

Managing your time and meeting deadlines. You will have to be organised in order to plan your assignment and meet other deadlines you may have, both inside and outside of school. If you are completing a production, you will have to fulfil many roles, both technical and non-technical, from pre-production through to post-production. This will require very tight scheduling and planning deadlines if you are to finish on time. You will have to prioritise and make ruthless decisions and you will learn very quickly to become disciplined in your approach to both your analysis and creation work.

Technical skills. During the analysis parts of the course you will closely examine the use of technical codes, and during the production stage (if you complete your assignment through to a stage of full development) it is very likely that you will have to use technical equipment of some sort. Rather than shy away from this element of the course you should try to learn as much as you can – there are plenty of tutorials on YouTube.

Critical analysis. The skills you will learn during the analysis sections of your course will ensure that you develop the mindset and knowledge to challenge your thinking. You will no longer accept viewpoints presented to you without careful consideration. The world will look a little different from your new, informed perspective.

Communication skills. As mentioned are central to media studies. You will have to employ active listening skills, develop your negotiation and persuasive skills, hone your people skills and learn to write clearly and convincingly.

Confidence! Your confidence will increase when you work with others to achieve a shared goal. If you have the chance, you should volunteer to act (or at least appear as a supporting artist), agree to be interviewed or offer to do some interviewing. This will really be a big boost to your confidence. Even if it feels daunting at first.

Routes of progression

There are many routes of progression once you have completed a National 5 award in media. If you have enjoyed the course, you could progress to Higher Media. There are numerous college courses and university degree programmes that you can consider. The most obvious are film, radio, television and journalism, although there are many other areas of creative media industries. Additionally, you could consider working in marketing, advertising, public relations, publishing, theatre and arts, the local government or teaching. Most large businesses will employ someone who is media savvy to deal with the public-relations (as well as create press releases) in their communications department.

ONLINE

Visit the Digital Zone at www.brightredbooks.net/subjects for tips on how to enhance your research skills; master time management; establish a good set of guidelines for group work and links to further media education and employers in Scotland.

DON'T FORGET

Even if you will be producing your own assignment, you should always talk to others about any challenges or creative ideas you may have. Working collaboratively is a great skill or habit to foster. Two (or more) heads are always better than one and some of the best creative projects have been an amalgamation of just that. You could also talk to your teachers or previous pupils about how they overcame obstacles such as no/low budget or juggling media projects with other subjects – you are not alone.

INTRODUCING NATIONAL 5 MEDIA
COURSE OUTLINE

ABOUT THIS BOOK

This guide is designed to help support you through your N5 Media Studies course and additionally serve as a good foundation for Higher Media (should you choose to take this route). The contents of the guide closely mirror the content and structure of the course in order to support your class work. You will learn about key aspects by working your way through the chapters. In order to deepen your understanding, you will have to apply your knowledge to unfamiliar content – the online sections are designed to support you to do just that. You do not have to work through the guide in any particular order, but you should complete all of the key aspects before you proceed to other sections as described below.

ABOUT THE COURSE

The National 5 course is made up of two parts – both requiring the same knowledge and understanding and both completely interdependent:

- Creation and production
- Analysis and evaluation

Both components are assessed externally by the Scottish Qualifications Authority (SQA) as follows:

1. The Question paper (exam)
2. The Assignment (you will work on this aspect for a substantial part of the year before it is sent away to be assessed)

There are no additional requirements for this course although your teacher may wish you to sit additional units as extra practice. To gain a National 5 award you must pass both parts of the course – your final result will be graded A–D.

Assignment (60 marks)

You will carry out an assignment set by SQA, using a given brief. There are two parts to this – a planning portfolio and a development stage where you will produce your content. You will also select elements of your content that you feel worked particularly well and evaluate areas that perhaps didn't work so well. All of this is described in detail in the relevant sections.

The exam (60 marks)

The exam component is two hours long and consists of five questions that allow you to demonstrate your knowledge and understanding of the key aspects of media literacy by applying them to content you have studied and by analysing an unseen print text so that the examiner can assess your understanding in an unfamiliar **context**. All of the sections in this book have been designed to show you how each key aspect may be presented to you, and assessed, in the exam. If you complete all of the practice questions on a regular basis, with a range of different texts, you will be very well prepared for the exam.

The language of media studies may be unfamiliar to you now, but you will soon get used to it: there is a glossary of key terms at the back of the book to help you. Although it may feel like hard work, you must always stop and further explore anything you don't understand before you proceed. The key aspects are relatively simple to grasp but a deeper understanding can only come from applying your knowledge and understanding in an unfamiliar context (in other words to unfamiliar texts). This will take time and commitment from you but should be a very rewarding experience and time well spent as you see your efforts reflected in the final examination results.

contd

Introducing National 5 Media – Course outline

The seven 'key aspects' that we teach in media are: categories, language, narrative, representation, institution, society and audience.

The first four (categories, language, narrative and representation) are what we call content-based key aspects – they all relate to the content evident in the text you are looking at. The last three (institution, society and audience) require you to consider context. You will look beyond the immediate text and consider, for example, the influencing factors or circumstances of the creating company; or the way a text is shaped by audience or reflects society in some way. You should work through these chapters carefully to make sure you understand the concepts and then use the suggestions as a guide to help you to put your knowledge into practice. The key aspects are explored in as much detail as space allows, and online content and tasks will ensure consolidation and development of your skills.

The key aspects work together to create meaning and purpose and your first job should be to learn what they are; they will become the tools you need in order to analyse and create content.

Key Aspect	Example
Categories	**Genre**, purpose, **tone**, medium, form, style
Language	Medium/Form-specific technical codes, **cultural codes**, anchorage
Narrative	Medium/Form-specific structures, codes, **conventions**
Representation	Selection and portrayal, **stereotypes**, **non-stereotypes**, cultural assumptions, **ideologies**

Key Aspects – Contexts	Example
Audience	Target audience, preferred reading, different audience reactions
Institution	Internal factors, external factors
Society	Time, place (for example, facts, information, ideas, historical portrayals, circumstances, events, politics, technology or any other societal factors relevant to the time the content was made, consumed or set)

Adapted from National 5 Course Specification, SQA, August 2017 edition, version 2.0

> **DON'T FORGET**
>
> This is a guide; your teacher will want to teach you using their own choice of texts and will have lots of additional material to prepare you for your exam. The guide is designed to consolidate your knowledge and help you to independently deepen your knowledge of media studies.

ROLE OF THE MEDIA

Central to the study of media is understanding the role of the media in society. Even if you have studied media in your English class previously you may not have considered the 'bigger picture'. There are lots of theories associated with this aspect of media – some of the more common ones are included in these sections, and suggestions for further study are online. Although these theories will at first be unfamiliar, they are interesting and will really help you understand how media content 'works'.

The roles of the media that we study in National 5 media are:

'Meeting Needs – to entertain, educate or inform.

Influencing attitudes and behaviours both intentional and unintentional

For a particular purpose: profit, self-interest or public service'. (SQA).

These are all explained fully in the relevant sections.

Throughout the course you will be introduced to a range of different texts to illustrate all of the above – they may include film posters; special interests; health and lifestyle; advertisements (for example, for fashion, beauty and cosmetics, cars, music and technology); TV dramas; news items.

>
> **ONLINE**
>
> To get the most out of this guide you should do all the extension work online at www.brightredbooks.net/subjects. Some of the online material is challenging and is excellent preparation for your exam and beyond. Good luck!

THINGS TO DO AND THINK ABOUT

Before you begin, take the time to familiarise yourself with both the key aspects and the role of the media concepts listed above.

INTRODUCING NATIONAL 5 MEDIA

CATEGORIES

When we consider the content-based key aspect of 'categories' in media studies, we refer to: medium, form, genre, purpose, style and tone.

MEDIUM AND FORM

In media, we refer to the way that the content is both presented to us and categorised. For example, if the medium is print the form could be a newspaper, poster or magazine. We could go one step further and identify the *genre* (see below) or type.

ACTIVITY: Copy and complete the following:

Medium	Examples of Form
Television	
Print	
Radio	
Film	

GENRE, STYLE AND TONE

The word *genre* refers to recognisable and repeated traits (specific to the form) that we are then able to classify. Different genres are often created through different narrative types and representations and these, in turn, are created using different types of cultural codes or form specific language codes.

So, if the *medium* is film and the *form* 'short narrative film', the *genre* could be 'social realism'; the purpose could be to entertain. The *style* determines the tone (typical elements of realism such as hand-held camera work, use of non-actors, minimal scripting and real settings may be used). The *style* could also be serious.

Understanding of genre helps both media producers and audience alike to have a common understanding of the expectations associated with each.

Genre can be classified and recognised in a number of different ways, such as having a recognisable *narrative structure* typical to form (see Narrative, pp. 26–31). It could also be a recognisable *setting*, for example, war films, road movies, historical dramas or westerns. Perhaps it might be **themes** that have evolved from science fiction or crime or a certain *tone*, such as comedy, **film noir** or horror. It may be a particular *target audience*, such as chic flic or teen film or a particular *production size*, such as low-budget film or blockbuster. *Genres* can combine and create *sub-genres*, for example: docudrama, romantic-comedy or action-comedy.

Tone is closely linked to genre and tells us how the writers feel about the subject or content. For example, you wouldn't expect a comedy to have a particularly serious tone or a documentary on a serious subject to have a flippant or comedic tone. A comedy would most likely be upbeat, entertaining and possibly light-hearted and informal while a documentary could be serious, formal and conventional.

THE BLURRING OF BOUNDARIES – GENERIC HYBRIDITY

Now that we are familiar with the basic concepts of genre and tone, let's take this one step further. Producers of media content will use recognisable genre conventions so that they can satisfy audience expectations, but they will also want to challenge audience expectations by combining different elements of genre such as setting, narrative conventions and iconography. This fusion of different elements of various genres is what is known as **generic hybridity**. A **hybrid** (or cross-genre) refers to the fusion of elements

contd

from two or more different genres. This form allows experimentation and is how new genres develop. It is not a new concept but is central to the evolution of new media.

COMEDY VÉRITÉ

The Office can be considered to be a hybrid genre called comedy vérité – a blend of the traditional ingredients of a sitcom with characteristics typical of reality TV (the reality TV genre fuses typical characteristics of both the documentary and drama genre). Other examples include: *Extras*, *Summer Heights High* and *This Time with Alan Partridge*. Historically, documentary and comedy were very separate and not often blended – unlike drama and comedy.

The following elements are typical of comedy vérité:
- The use of narrative techniques such as direct address (characters who acknowledge the camera) and a more 'informal' camera style.
- A balance between ongoing 'serial style' **story arcs** of drama and those of a more self-contained sitcom **series** with each **episode** standing alone and concluding in a satisfactory way (see page 31 on narrative in TV drama).
- Lead characters who are a blend of typical flawed characters from sitcom and real-life participants from documentary/docudrama programmes.
- An incongruous (unusual) mismatch between drama and reality. The blending of comedy and the reality style interaction with audience or programme makers and crew (for example, *Mrs. Brown's Boys* and *This Time with Alan Partridge*) that often creates an awkward humour.

PURPOSE

The purpose of content is most often to make some profit but, of course, this isn't always the case (see Role of the Media, pp. 38–47, for examples). Purpose could be to:
- meet audience needs (inform/educate, such as a documentary, or to entertain)
- achieve an institutional purpose (profit, promotion or public service)
- influence attitudes and behaviour (intentionally or unintentionally, for example, government public information films such as alcohol-awareness campaigns).

The link between categories and the context-based key aspect of audience is a strong one. Different genres share different characteristics, and audiences will both recognise and expect the content they choose to be true to form and to meet the expectations of their chosen genre. Their expectations and needs will have to be met if the production (or content) is to be a success. So, genre, tone, style and purpose are all very closely linked. The producers know that they can't subvert (change or challenge) the genre too much because fans may not like it, which means they may not make the profit they need to. Although some audiences, for example, fans of *arthouse films*, enjoy being challenged and surprised.

 ONLINE

Read more about hybridity in TV sit com at www.brightredbooks.net/subjects

 DON'T FORGET

Deliberate references to other kinds of media text (intertextuality) can also include examples such as the adaptation of a novel (set, for example, in the 1800s but given a modern-day setting (combining elements of different time periods)).

 DON'T FORGET

Remember that although the key aspects are interrelated, *purpose* is a good starting point. All media texts are shaped by purpose.

 ONLINE

Head to the Digital Zone for more practice and an example of an exam-style question on genre – www.brightredbooks.net/subjects

 ## THINGS TO DO AND THINK ABOUT

Complete the table below. Try to explore as many examples as you can.

Medium	Form	Genre and Possible Genre Conventions	Style and Tone	Purpose
Print media				
Radio				
Film	Full-length feature	Action – chase **scenes**, high-action, fast-paced adventure, such as disasters, fight sequences, Propp's character types, Todorov's narrative structure	Style (depending on director). Possible fast-paced editing sequences, standard camera set-ups (establishing **shot** closing into action), **continuity editing**. Upbeat, tense	To make profit for creating institution, To entertain/ For escapism
Television				
Internet				

 ONLINE TEST

Test yourself on categories at www.brightredbooks.net/subjects

LANGUAGE

CAMERA WORK

> **DON'T FORGET**
>
> In the next few chapters we will explore common **technical codes** and **conversions**. Combined they create meaning.

RECOGNISING CAMERA SHOTS

In any moving image, meaning is constructed by carefully combining a series of camera shots. Filming is an expensive business and nothing is left to chance so each frame is carefully selected to move the story forward. It is important that you can recognise key camera shots in the texts you are studying in order to understand and analyse how the director has constructed meaning. You should familiarise yourself with the correct technical terminology so that you can build a vocabulary for discussing your text with clarity and insight.

In this section you will be introduced to a number of camera shots – there are many more. The best way to familiarise yourself with them is to try and recognise as many as you can, as often as you can, in as many different genres as possible.

We can categorise camera work as follows:

- **Distance** or length of shot in relation to subject, for example: close-up or long shot.
- **Camera movement**, such as pan or track.
- **Camera angle**, for example: high or low angle.

Establishing shot.

Distance

Establishing shot or extreme long shot – Used to set the scene for the audience. There is usually very little detail in this type of shot, rather it gives a quick impression of location.

Long shot – Closer to the subject than the establishing shot and a general rule of thumb this would frame characters as full length and can still include plenty of background.

Medium shot – Usually frames a character from the waist up. Often used for dialogue scenes.

Close-up – This shot will show very little background and usually focuses on the face or a specific object in detail. The shot is highlighting the importance of something (or somebody) to the audience and often shows us character emotions.

Extreme close-up – As the name suggests, this frame closes in to reveal a shot which is generally magnified.

Camera Movement

Dolly Shots – A dolly shot moves smoothly towards, away from or alongside the subject without zooming in. A dolly (a cart which travels on tracks to create this effect) is a very expensive piece of equipment, although many filmmakers on a low or no budget film have made their own improvised dolly carts.

Pan – In a panning shot the camera is secured to a central point, for example a tripod, and scans around in a smooth sweeping motion.

Tilt – As above only at an angle.

Handheld – Used for many different effects, but often an unsteady camera can create a sense of realism as it is closer to the way we see the world.

Steadicam – A device used to isolate the camera from the operator and thus eliminate any unwanted jarring or jolting of the camera.

Close up.

> **ONLINE**
>
> Visit the Digital Zone at www.brightredbooks.net/subjects for examples of camera shots.

contd

Language – Camera work

Camera Angles

Birds Eye View – Shows a scene from overhead, which can distort everyday objects and make them appear unrecognisable. Can also give an overview of a scene.

High Angle – The camera is raised above the action, making the subject look smaller or less important. Usually taken from specialist equipment called a crane.

Eye Level – Often used to appear as if the camera were a character observing a scene.

Low Angle – The camera is positioned well below the eye-line of the character or object, making the character or object appear larger than life and often quite intimidating. This is often used as a trick to make smaller actors look bigger! A more extreme angle can remove much of the background detail, for example revealing sky if outside. This can be quite surreal for the audience.

Canted angle (Dutch tilt) – A tilted camera can suggest an instability or uncertainty in a character.

High angle.

THE IMPORTANCE OF CAMERA WORK

Camera work is a technical code and so falls under the heading of key aspects (language), however, this section will also become a useful frame of reference if you decide to make a moving-image text for the assignment part of your course. Expose yourself to as many different examples of camera work as you can – be inspired and experiment as much as possible to create your own individual style of filming.

As with all of the *content-based key aspects* you must avoid studying them in isolation but instead always try to both combine them and link them to the other *context-based key aspects* – institution, society and audience. Does an audience expect certain camera shots typical of the genre they are watching? Were their expectations met? Do certain directors have a recognisable or expected style? Have institutional **constraints** such as limitations on, or the availability of technology, had an impact on the finished product?

 **DON'T FORGET**

Once you are familiar with different camera shots and how they are used, the best way to familiarise yourself with the benefits of each are to film short sequences using different shots, as often as possible.

 ONLINE

You can download a template from www.brightredbooks.net to help you and also use it to analyse key scenes from texts you are studying.

THINGS TO DO AND THINK ABOUT

Watch any clip of a TV programme or film and stop the film at as many points as you can.

1. Try to describe the type of shot in terms of camera framing, movement and angles.

2. Explain the reason you think the director chose that particular shot. In other words, what is the effect?

3. Research a well-known film or TV director and see if you can identify any similarities between examples of their works. What were the institutional constraints placed upon the production and what effect did it have on the final production? How did the target audience influence the content of the production?

4. Once you are relatively familiar with a variety of camera work you can storyboard your own short film or scene.

If you are stuck for ideas, pick from one of the following themes: *freedom, poverty, pressure, success* or *isolation*. Alternatively, you could think of a novel, play or poem you know well and try to adapt a scene from the text by creating a storyboard. Be creative; adaptations often only capture the main ideas (or themes) of the original story. For this mini-film, you should try to use about ten carefully selected shots, without dialogue. If time allows you can shoot your story, play it to the rest of the class and see if they can guess what your theme was. This is also useful for evaluating the process prior to working on your unit assessment and final assignment. You will find further advice in the assignment chapter towards the end of the book.

 ONLINE

Follow the link at www.brightredbooks.net for an example of a real storyboard from *Poldark*.

 ONLINE TEST

Test yourself on camera work at www.brightredbooks.net

LANGUAGE
EDITING

TECHNICAL CODES: THE EDITING PROCESS

Editing is the process of piecing together sections of moving image to create a series of scenes so that they create meaning. Often the clips flow seamlessly from shot to shot, however, editing can have many different uses and produce many different effects.

The editor works closely with the director and is responsible for making sure each shot is carefully chosen to create the final story.

CONTINUITY EDITING

Continuity editing is a process where one shot continues on from another to produce a clear narrative. The scenes will be decoded easily by the audience as they closely mimic reality.

A *cut* is where two different shots have been joined together. Quite often in continuity editing the cuts are so smooth that we hardly notice. The following are typical examples of ways of editing shots into a basic sequence.

Establishing shot – a long shot showing enough of the scene for the audience to understand the setting (sets the scene).

Match on action – that is, a character throws a punch, for example, towards another and the editor matches the shot exactly with the receiver of the punch falling backward – this will look seamless and the audience won't question it.

Match on sound – perhaps we hear a ship's horn in the first shot; if that sound continues over into the next shot the audience immediately knows we are in the same location – extremely useful and also known as the sound bridge.

Shot–reverse–shot – two people are having a conversation facing each other and the camera switches from one to the other (often called over-the-shoulder shot).

Eye-line match – character looks at an object and the editor then cuts to a view of that object so we know what it is. They may return to the character for a reaction shot (think *Titanic* when the crew member first spots the iceberg!).

180° rule – if you are attempting the above you have to imagine an imaginary line between your characters and ensure that you stay on one side. If you 'cross the line' your character will suddenly appear on the wrong side of the screen and your audience will be very confused!

DON'T FORGET

If you are considering storyboarding or producing a film for your assignment it is worth considering different ways that you can create meaning through various styles of editing. It is relatively simple to do on a basic package, such as Windows Movie Maker or iMovie, and once you have the basics you can be really creative. Some believe the basic process of editing originated in 1898 by British filmmaker Robert W. Paul, in his film *Come Along, Do!* This was refined by D. W. Griffith who developed a more sophisticated technique called 'parallel editing'.

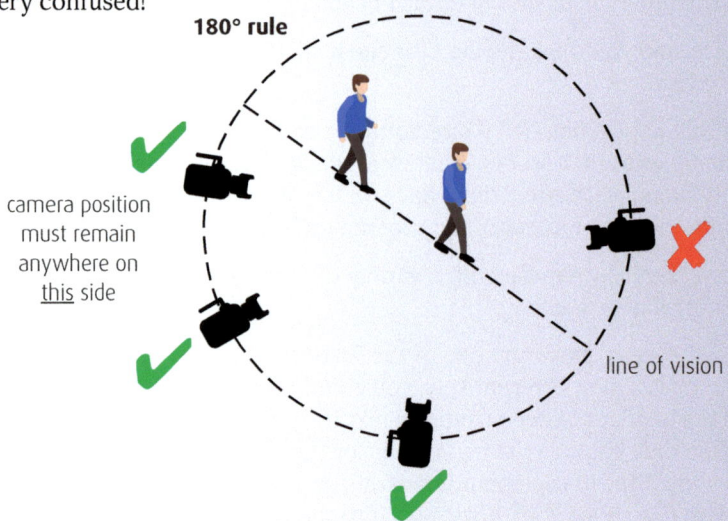

The 180° rule.

Language – Editing

30° rule – The 30° rule suggests that you must have at least 30° difference in angle from the last shot or essentially it will be too similar – and there will not be enough new information in the shot for the audience. It will still be seamless though. Any more and you have created a jump cut. The audience will then focus on the editing more than your story so it is worth avoiding unless you mean to do it.

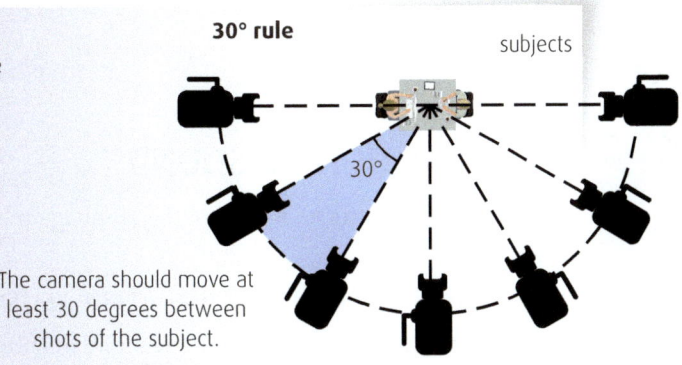

The camera should move at least 30 degrees between shots of the subject.

The 30° rule.

NON-CONTINUITY EDITING

Non-continuity editing, in contrast, aims to disrupt the narrative in order to create a specific effect not usually in chronological order. Examples of this style of editing would be **'montage'** and the inclusion of **'flashback'** type narratives.

Montage was made famous by early Soviet filmmaker and graduate of the Moscow Film School director Sergei Eisenstein, as an illusion to suggest a story. It can be best described as a series of images edited together to create a new story, often used to build tension and condense time. Eisenstein's 1925 Russian propaganda film *Battleship Potemkin* boasts one of the most famous montage sequences of all time, 'The Odessa steps sequence', which has been referenced in films such as *The Untouchables* by Brian De Palma (1987). The sequence shows the extent of the violence of the revolution through a number of apparently unrelated shots of men, women and children being trampled and shot, and during the climax of the film a baby in a pram teeters precariously at the top of the stairs. The shots are pieced together, and the illusion of violence and chaos of the scene is perfectly portrayed.

American montage

American montage is a series of shots often using dissolves, again to compress time. Look at the 1949 version of *The Great Gatsby*, where it is used to give an impression of the bootlegging and organised crime in the 1920s. Another good example is the training montage from 1982 *Rocky III*, showing the gruelling training regime of Stallone.

Alfred Hitchcock's shower scene in the film *Psycho* (1960) is another good example. Poor Marion is brutally attacked in a shower in her hotel room by the disturbed Norman Bates. The scene was considered graphic for the time and yet the whole thing was an illusion. The audience never once see the knife stabbing her body (the sound effect was in fact a knife stabbing a melon). Different angles of Marion in the shower were edited together to evoke the sense of panic and disorientation felt by Marion in the last moments of her life.

French New Wave filmmakers such as Jean-Luc Godard did not conform to Hollywood editing styles and used editing to challenge the audience.

THINGS TO DO AND THINK ABOUT

There are many different editing cuts and transitions and it would be impossible to list them all here. There are some excellent examples on the Internet, and it would be worth spending some time researching these techniques. This information can be used for the planning part of your assignment so make sure you keep detailed notes. Done well, these are fantastic tools for enhancing a narrative – but overdo them and again you risk ruining your film entirely.

VIDEO LINK

Watch the complete sequence that has been re-scored by the Pet Shop Boys on the Digital Zone – www.brightredbooks.net/subjects

VIDEO LINK

Watch the clip of À *bout de souffle* (*Breathless*) (1960) by Godard on the Digital Zone and watch how he uses jump cuts to disorientate his audience.

DON'T FORGET

Experiment, don't over-use transitions and learn the basic rules of continuity editing. Make sure you can identify them before you start experimenting with different types of non-continuity editing.

VIDEO LINK

Watch the scene where Chrissie has her last swim in the cult classic *Jaws* (1975) on the BrightRED Digital Zone and complete an extra activity on editing!

ONLINE

Visit www.brightredbooks.net/subjects for extra activities and tips on this topic!

ONLINE TEST

Test your knowledge of editing at www.brightredbooks.net/subjects

LANGUAGE
SOUND

THE FUNCTION OF SOUND

Sound is a very powerful aspect of the language of moving images and serves a variety of functions:

- to support (or contrast with) the *narrative* and reinforce meaning
- to act as a *sound bridge* linking one scene to another (such as would be a typical characteristic of *continuity editing*)
- to make a scene more believable
- to create tone such as fear or comedy
- to anchor our understanding of meaning
- to allow character dialogue or **voice-over**
- to add a *narrative* perspective, that is, character voice-over
- to act as a *non-diegetic metaphor*
- to hold together a *montage sequence*

Leitmotif is a repeated phrase or theme used to suggest an idea or character. An iconic example would be John Williams' score 'The Imperial March (Darth Vader's Theme)' (*Star Wars: Episode V – The Empire Strikes Back*, Irvin Kershner, 1980).

DON'T FORGET

A noticeable lack of sound can emphasise the visual elements and convey a very powerful message. Try this in your own work.

DIEGETIC AND NON-DIEGETIC

Sound can be described as being either **diegetic** or **non-diegetic**.

Simply put, *diegetic* means that we hear what the character hears and can see the source of the sound such as character dialogue, cars screeching, loud explosions or a window smashing. *Non-diegetic* refers to sound we hear, but the character doesn't, such as a soundtrack or subtle sound effects. The background ticking throughout Christopher Nolan's film *Dunkirk* (2017) could be considered a metaphor for the soldiers running out of time.

Sound should enhance the meaning of a particular scene or storyline so that the audience expects, accepts and understands its use without question.

A well-chosen soundtrack can add a powerful and emotive tone to a moving-image production and instantaneously pull your audience through a range of emotions. From heart-wrenching and haunting melodies such as those in *Titanic*, *Into the Wild*, *The Last of the Mohicans* and *The Lord of the Rings* to big powerful orchestral numbers such as we would expect from Bond theme tunes like 'Diamonds are Forever' by Dame Shirley Bassey and 'Skyfall' by singer Adele. In contrast, a sinister strings soundtrack can provide 'edge-of-your-seat' suspense, for example, the iconic theme tune to *Halloween*, *Insidious* or *Candyman*.

 ACTIVITY

Look at the following examples of possible tones: complete the table and add some examples of your own.

Genre/Form	Identifiable Tone through Music/Sound
Daytime chat shows	Upbeat/Friendly
Prime-time news programme	Dramatic
Sit com	
Horror movie	
Romantic comedy	

contd

Language – Sound

EXAMPLE:

Look at the following example which has been answered in detail, using an example of sound from the British war film *Dunkirk* directed by Christopher Nolan. Try to answer the same question using a different example of sound in film. Remember to develop your points.

Q *'The tone of a text conveys a particular mood or feeling.'*

A) From a text you have studied describe one or more examples of tone. 2

B) Explain how the tone you have identified in part (a) has been created using technical or cultural codes. 6

SOLUTION:

Answer A

The British war film *Dunkirk* evokes a tone of immense tension and despair for the audience as they witness several key characters desperately trying to escape the beaches of Dunkirk in order to return to the safety of British shores.

Answer B

The narrative in *Dunkirk* is relatively basic, told from the perspective of three soldiers trying to flee Dunkirk from air, sea and land. Nolan uses sound to hold together the three storylines and create an immersive cinematic experience for the audience.

Dialogue in the film is minimal and as an audience, we expect to hear dialogue over sound. Nolan uses the *diegetic* sounds of war to drown out the dialogue of his key characters. Dramatic echoes of exploding bombs, the sinister sound of approaching enemy aircraft and torpedoes all create tension, as seen throughout the beach scenes. This helps the audience to better experience the horror of the situation; the emotions of the soldiers are felt by the audience without need for dialogue.

Non-diegetic

The soundtrack to the film was composed by Hans Zimmer (who worked with Nolan on films such as *Inception* (2010), *The Dark Knight* (2008), *The Dark Knight Rises* (2012) and *Interstellar* (2014). Zimmer uses a technique known as the 'Shepard Tone', which is described as an 'audio illusion' by Nolan and refers to the impression of a constant *ascending* pitch.

Zimmer created the sound by layering three different tones on a track and fading out the top pitch so that the middle and bottom two can continue – this continues on a loop, which gives a seamless impression of a pitch that rises to screaming point and continues to do so throughout the film. Also used in *The Dark Knight* and *Interstellar*, this unsettling and *discordant* sound unsettles the audience and reinforces the building tension.

In addition, layered over the 'Shepard Tone', the ticking sound of a clock is audible throughout the film, serving as a constant reminder that time is running out for the soldiers as the likelihood of escape becomes improbable. This helps us constantly anticipate the worse outcome for the characters. Finally, towards the end of the film the surviving soldiers are set against a backdrop of normal everyday sounds. This marks the end of the horror.

THINGS TO DO AND THINK ABOUT

You could choose any other aspect of language from the film to complete the question in accordance with the number of marks available. Remember, you can use more than one text in your answer.

DON'T FORGET

In the exam you should refer to a range of codes as it is likely that several have been used to convey meaning.

ONLINE

Visit the Digital Zone for support with adding sound to your assignment production and to find a link to download Audacity.

ONLINE

Find research tasks, links, activities and examples at www.brightredbooks.net/subjects

ONLINE TEST

Test yourself on this topic on the Digital Zone!

15

LANGUAGE

LIGHTING

LIGHT UP, LIGHT UP

Lighting is used in both stills photography (such as for use in advertising) and moving image. Firstly, for practical reasons (because the camera can't quite see everything that the eye can see) and, secondly, for creatively conveying mood and effect.

You should read this section and analyse examples of lighting in the texts you are studying as well as researching other examples of media content where lighting is used for effect. As well as analysing the use of lighting in preparation for the question paper section of your exam, you may also want to consider how you will use lighting in your assignment. Remember, content such as a magazine advertisements or film posters will all use lighting to help convey mood and meaning.

Usually, lighting is invisible to the audience, meaning that the lights are placed out of shot yet still illuminating the scene as required. Some sources of light are placed 'in shot', for example, a table lamp or a candle – these are sometimes called 'practicals'. Again, this is something you may want to use in your own production. Where budget allows, most exterior shots will be lit by huge halogen lamps, both to ensure continuity (as the weather and time of day change the intensity of the light) and also to extend shooting hours.

The classic Hollywood three-point lighting set-up is standard and can be used to light your subject in a flattering way. Although there are variations, typically the main light or '*key light*' is used to light the subject from about 45 per cent above and off-centre.

A *fill light* is used to eliminate distracting or unsightly shadows and is usually placed on the opposite side of the camera to the key light – its purpose is to bounce light back onto the subject. You can easily make a reflector out of white, gold or silver card, depending on the effect you require. Reflectors are relatively cheap to buy and an essential piece of kit – should you be doing lots of filming or photography.

A *back light* – sometimes called a rim or halo light – is placed out of sight to add *depth* to the frame, so that the *foreground* is separated from the *background*, making your subject 'pop'. If you don't use a backlight your scene could appear too 'flat', which is unrealistic. In reality our world has depth, and three-point lighting will add interest and look professional.

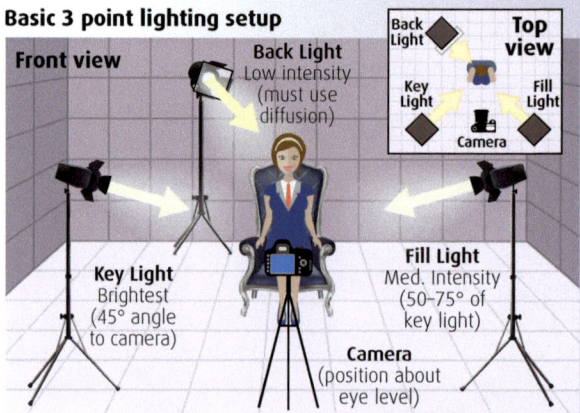

Examples of different lighting set-ups.

Assignment tip

If you are filming or using photography (unless you have access to an expensive lighting kit) you will have to be creative with what you have available. This sometimes produces very interesting effects and will give you key points for discussion during your planning stage, as a lack of budget may have resulted in a lack of equipment and therefore require you to explore other options. This is an example of an *internal institutional constraint*. Even if you are not taking your assignment to full production stage, you can still plan your lighting. Allow yourself to be inspired by content you have studied.

Language – Lighting

LIGHTING FOR EFFECT

 DON'T FORGET

Don't forget to use natural lighting. Available light from a window, for example, can bounce onto your subject using a reflector.

Now that you know the basics you can play around with your lighting set-up and get creative. The possibilities are endless, and you should spend some time researching different effects. Here are some to start you off.

Placement of the *key light* at a low angle, looking up at your subject, will throw unusual shadows upwards across the face, giving your subject an unnatural disturbing and almost supernatural feel.

Placing the key light at one side of your subject will almost wash out one side of the face while throwing the other side into darkness. This is sometimes called *chiaroscuro lighting* and can be very effective in lots of situations, for example, to suggest a mysterious side or uncertainty in your character. Lighting is a key marker of the *film noir* genre, which reflected the dark insecurities of a post-war period – an antidote to the optimisms reflected in Hollywood musicals and films.

You can create a silhouette effect by placing the key light behind the subject.

 ONLINE

Learn more about lighting from the BBC Academy and find further examples on the Digital Zone – www.brightredbooks.net/subjects

 **ACTIVITY**

Look at examples of film noir and identify examples of dramatic lighting.

 THINGS TO DO AND THINK ABOUT

Remember – as a student of media, it is not enough just to identify the style of lighting used and the effect. You have to go one step further and consider the relationship between other key aspects, for example, when answering the following question:

1 Describe how the language (cultural and technical codes) in content you have studied has met the expectations of the audience?

An example you could draw on could be as follows:

> Low-key lighting is an expected convention of the thriller genre as it adds to the suspense element. Martin Scorsese's film Shutter Island is a good example. When protagonist Teddy Daniels searches the cells in Ward C, which housed the most dangerous patients, very low-key lighting is used to create a dark, shadowy and gloomy atmosphere. The dark scene is unnerving; we feel his vulnerability as he can't see what is around him and nor can we. This adds to the eeriness of the mental institution and makes the audience feel on edge as it puts them in the position of the character (in this case – in the dark).

Now, try your own example from content you have studied.

 ONLINE TEST

Test yourself on this topic at www.brightredbooks.net/subjects

LANGUAGE

PRINT LANGUAGE

ANALYSING A PRINT TEXT

DON'T FORGET

It may be helpful to revise the persuasive language techniques you have learned in English (to help you with your RUAE and writing folio) as this could help you to analyse your print text too. You will find a reminder on page 20 if you need it.

In your National 5 exam you will be asked to analyse a print text. You will choose from either a film promotion poster, an advert or a magazine cover. Once you have learned the basic principles of analysing adverts you should practice with as many examples as you can find in preparation for the exam. You do not need to be familiar with the content of the texts – there may be celebrities or actors you do not recognise or a product you have never heard of – don't worry! While it may be useful to consider any prior knowledge you have to your answer, there will be more than enough content for you to work through in your answer. The advertisements will have been chosen very carefully and will be rich in content; the key is to be really observant and know what to look for. Work through the following unit before attempting your own analysis.

TYPOGRAPHY

The use of language is crucial in advertising. Equally as important, if a little more subtle, is the *typography*, which is the way the text is arranged on the page to make it easy to read and the style used to make it attractive to the reader.

The following is a list of basic terms that may also help you with the layout of your own text (should you choose to use print medium for your assignment). The typography of an advert should create interest, reinforce a message or theme, reveal emotion and look good!

Elements of typography

Typeface refers to the design style – such as: Helvetica, **Rockwell condensed** or Times New Roman. Often, they set the theme; they could be, for example: childlike, *elegant*, formal or *dictate a certain period in history*.

Font traditionally refers to the weight and size such as 12, 14, 16 or 18. Italics is also a font.

> *Tracking* – refers to the spaces between words.
> *Kerning* – refers to the white spaces between the letters.
> *Leading* – is the measurement between, above and below lines.
> *Line length* – is self-explanatory!

The colour of the text is also an important consideration as different colours can have different **connotations**.

 ACTIVITY

Thinking about all of the options available to you, create a poster advertising one of the following: a local music festival, a service promoting support of mental health issues in teens, a careless driving awareness event or another event of your choice. You will consider your audience and purpose before considering the choices of print language available to you. You should annotate your poster justifying the choices you have made.

Serifs are the small lines at the end of characters.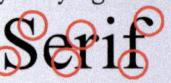

Sans is French for 'without'. Sans serif means 'without lines'.

Sans Serif		Serif
Thought to be harder to read		Eye naturally follows the text so easier to read
Good for headlines	VERSUS	Good for larger amounts of text such as books and magazines
Often used in advertising		Most commonly used font in books, magazines and any lengthy text
Good for web designs		
Easier for visually impaired or children to read		
Considered more modern and informal		

 ONLINE

Head to www.brightredboooks.net/subjects for a task on the connotations of colour.

contd

If you are creating your own print, do play around with different styles of text and see what effects work for you. You can create a visual hierarchy by separating different sections with different styles of text. If the most important text were the heaviest, it would clearly stand out.

ADVERTISING

Gender stereotyping

Key to creating an effective advertisement is the use of the gender stereotype to promote desirable *ideologies* (a particular view of the world). For example, female stereotypes could suggest an inequality to the male. They may appear weaker or perhaps conform to an exaggerated or unrealistic feminine appearance. They may be *objectified* and exist for the *male gaze*. Male stereotypes often act in a 'typically' manly way, appearing tough and in control, often being shown as the family breadwinner.

There are four common categories of gender stereotypes:

- *Physical appearance* – women are often unrealistically represented as petite and men as tall with a strong physique.
- *Personality traits* – for example, women portrayed as demure and passive, clean and tidy and the main organisers. Men are often shown as tough, strong, dominant and self-assured.
- *Occupations* – typically include women performing domestic, caring, nurturing or supporting jobs (such as teaching, nursing, secretarial roles or housewives) and men boasting physical, intelligent or powerful jobs, such as firemen, engineers, politicians, scientists or doctors. Men are often higher earners than women.
- *Domestic behaviours* – women are often seen in the kitchen, doing housework or looking after children, whereas men might be doing domestic repairs or other typically masculine activities.

ACTIVITY

Look at the following four pictures and see how many of the above categories you can use to describe the stereotype.

THINGS TO DO AND THINK ABOUT

Find examples of adverts that contain gender stereotypes: complete the table below for each example.

What is being advertised and where did you find it?	What is the stereotype and how is it created? Consider images, representations, typography, colour and so forth.	Why is the representation effective in helping the advert meet its needs?	How is it effective in meeting the needs of the audience?	Why might the representation be considered problematic? Consider groups of the public that may be offended.	Who do you think are the target audience for this advert? Why?

DON'T FORGET

Stereotypes vary according to culture. Some of the stereotypes presented in this book would not be understood by other cultures (or even some audiences within our own culture). Always consider and research your target audience thoroughly.

ONLINE TEST

Test your knowledge of this topic at www.brightredbooks.net/subjects

LANGUAGE

PERSUASION AND EMOTIVE LANGUAGE

PERSUASIVE TECHNIQUES FOR ADVERTISING

As well as looking at the colour and type of font, it is helpful to identify any of the techniques below evident in the text as this will reinforce (or question) the purpose.

Technique	How it Works	Persuasive Effect
Emotive language or Pathos	Words loaded with sentiment for effect. Appealing to the emotions of the audience.	Words such as 'suffering', 'vulnerable', 'defenceless' and 'powerless'.
Rhetorical question	Question posed to the reader to convince them there is no other answer than the one they offer. So not really a question because it does not expect an answer – it expects or hopes for agreement without question – very convincing.	Questions the reader in a way that persuades them the author is right or an authority on the subject. 'Do you really need to spend all your time scrubbing the bath when Magic Mousse can do it in half the time?'
Statistics	Numbers used to back up evidence. Usually manipulated to persuade. Four out of ten sounds weaker than 'as many as 40 per cent'.	More than 60 per cent of those we asked reported an improvement in their symptoms. Adds apparent credibility.
Direct address	For example, by addressing the audience by using personal pronouns: I, you, he, she, it, we, they, me, him, her, us, and them.	Second-person pronoun – 'you'. The audience are involved as they are being spoken to directly. Their opinion matters. Problems become their problems. 'Do you need faster Internet connection speed'?
Hyperbole	Exaggeration often teamed with superlatives such as biggest, hottest and best.	Attempts to convince the target audience that, for example, the product is far superior to any other: 'This is by far the best book on the market.'
Rule of three	When words are put together and grouped into threes, the phrase becomes memorable and powerful, especially if it is sharp and concise.	For example: 'Online shopping that's fast, convenient and secure'. '*Veni, vidi, vici*' (I came, I saw, I conquered)' – Julius Caesar. Or BLT – 'Bacon, lettuce and tomato'. These phrases are all memorable.
Imperatives or commands	Literally command the target audience to take action.	'Check out the website below for more information.' 'Sit down. Put your feet up. Have a coffee.' (Note that this also employs the rule of three.)
Weasel words	Purposely vague claims or statements. A modifier that, at first, appears convincing and suggests credibility but lacks conviction on closer inspection. Usually anonymous.	This product <u>may</u> help if used as part of a calorie-controlled diet. '<u>Virtually</u> eliminates spots.'
Unfinished claims	Part of a claim, again very vague.	'Gives you more …' Great, but more than what?

EMOTIVE LANGUAGE

As media students we learn to become experts at recognising the use of persuasive language in a text to convince or even entertain the target audience. With practice we can 'cut through' this language and realise that we are, in some way, being manipulated.

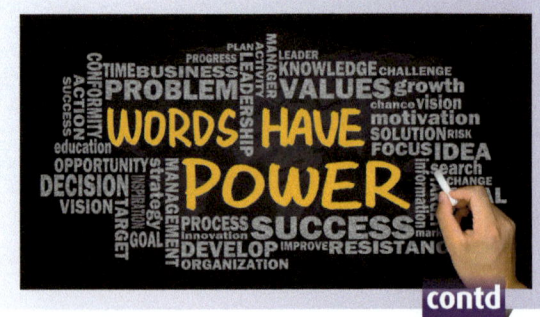

contd

Language – Persuasion and emotive language

What is emotive language?

A quick Google search of synonyms of 'emotive' reveals the following: 'sensitive, poignant, affecting, touching, moving and impassioned' (Office Word online synonym searcher). An audience needs to care about a story (or the topic of an advert) before they engage with the content. The use of language is crucial in helping them do so. Emotive words are loaded, meaning they are power words.

Why is emotive language used? Does it affect objectivity?

Emotive language affects objectivity – there is no way around this. The producers of content have to fight harder and harder for their audience. This is because we (the target audience) are drowning in a sea of information. We may be fed a news feed directly onto our mobile phones based on previous content we have selected. We are bombarded with content on every social media platform, with emails and in news media. Ultimately, we can choose which content we wish to engage with. We have access to more and more journalism content and we are spoiled for choice.

Emotive headline.

Can you see the problem that content producers face? Clearly, there is more competition now than ever before. Would you rather read content that was entertaining or lively or purely factual? Do you think it can be both?

Traditionally, news was reported 'post-event'. Now we can witness it as it happens. Think of shaky hand-held camera shots of by passers caught up in an event such as the Manchester bombing in 2017. We witnessed panic and disbelief as the horror unfolded in real time. In this type of reporting, we feel a part of the scene and we understand better the full horror of the situation. It is becoming harder and harder to compete for attention from a traditional newspaper.

Emotion is a tool designed to engage. It could come in the form of visuals such as live footage, or could be a case of writing in a style that is relatable. It taps into our needs. We are all human and the human element of any story is often what matters most to us. We respond to human-interest stories. 'Emotion' rather than facts. We are primarily 'feeling' beings. We need to 'relate' to a story whether visual or written.

THINGS TO DO AND THINK ABOUT

Thinking about the role of the media in our society, consider the following:

1. Do you think that news should be free of emotive language? Why?
2. Do you think that advertising should be free from emotive or persuasive language? In your groups discuss the above before sharing.
3. You may well need to manipulate language for effect in your own assignment work.
4. Research some loaded or emotive words now. Here are a few to help you.

Words that Provoke or Suggest Emotion	Words that Suggest Corruption	Action Words	To Evoke Curiosity
Fury, rage, resentment, outrage, indignation, hatred, bitterness, distressed, distraught, terrified, threatening, repulsive, shocking, harmful, malicious, violent, vindictive	Lying, abuse, corrupt, backstabbing, cowardly, hidden, secretive, illegal, unauthorised, mistrust	Now, only (that is, offer only valid for next 24 hours) easy, free, proven results, results	Secret, agenda, confidential, banned, off the record, hidden, concealed

ONLINE TEST

Head to the Digital Zone to test yourself on persuasion and emotive language!

REPRESENTATION

IDEOLOGIES

THE ROLE OF IDEOLOGIES

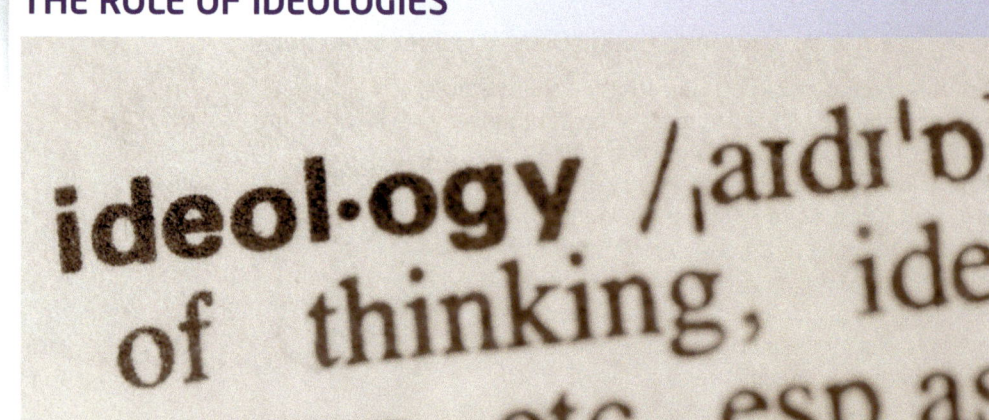

Ideologies are shared understandings of a set of values and beliefs. These ideologies are often decided for us and in turn presented to us by the media. As we know, the media reaches a mass audience and sometimes, as a result, people start to subscribe to (or support) these ideologies. We all live our lives by a set of ideologies and much of the time we fail to question them. In a way, it helps guide us to live by a set of values. Beliefs are usually shaped by institutions (large organisations) such as education, politics, the law and religion.

One example would be the idea of consumerism. This suggests that material goods will make us happier, better people. It is the basis on which the advertising industry is built. Our lives would be improved in some way if we had a newer car, the latest iPhone, more clothes, a bigger house or a better holiday. As a pupil of media studies, you should always try to recognise and challenge these beliefs!

When we talk about preferred reading or differential **decoding**, we mean that we can look at the text from different perspectives (for example, a feminist outlook). A group of people will usually hold a set of common beliefs about society or an aspect of society. These beliefs can shape our outlook on various aspects of society. We may accept or reject certain representations. It is important that we consider the viewpoints of others, even if they are not in line with our own beliefs, otherwise we would end up with a very unbalanced society.

Ideology and representation are closely linked in media studies because, in media content, these representations will convey messages about the views of the creating institution or assist us in revealing themes or issues being explored within the text. When studying a piece of text, you should consider whose views are being represented and, crucially, whose are not! Although this concept may feel unfamiliar and daunting at first, it would serve you well to do enough research to become a little more familiar with a few popular ideologies. With a little hard work, you will soon expand your understanding of some of these widely held beliefs and it would also be excellent preparation for Higher Media.

Representation – Ideologies

Knight and Pattison, in their book *British Politics for Dummies*, have summarised some of the main political ideas in a simple format for quick reference. Below are a few of them simplified further still. Try to add to the list. Researching this task would be time well spent, as depending on your assignment brief you could well explore and include your findings as part of your content research.

'ism' in Question	An Example of Media Content that Explores these Ideologies
Anarchism – as a result of societal issues such as poverty as a result of unemployment, economic situations of a country and so on. They are anti-government.	*Land and Freedom* (1995)
Capitalism – in a capitalist society individuals, people or companies operate for a profit.	*Charlie and the Chocolate Factory* (2005) *Limitless* (2011)
Communism. Communists oppose capitalist beliefs. They are often ordinary workers with concerns that capitalist society will be damaging to the masses. Key to the ideology they aim to limit exploitation of workers and the class system. Historically, revolutionary and involved in uprisings. There are many different factions of communism under the broad heading of Marxism. Not too different from socialism.	*Land and Freedom* (1995) Ken Loach
Conservatism. Holds in high regard traditions of the past such as government structures and education systems. Keen to uphold those aspects.	*American Sniper* (2014) Although a different reading could reveal a liberal stance.
Feminism – support equality in society for women, for example, equal pay scales. In media often concern themselves with derogatory representations of women.	*Thelma and Louise* (1991) *The Big Heat* (1953) *Miss Representation* (2011) *Juno* (2007) *Mulan* (1998)
Liberalism – belief in the freedom and rights of the individual. Fight to make things more competitive and fairer in the market place and that those without power have a voice and are not taken advantage of.	*Avatar* (2009) *Dead Poets Society* (1989) *To Kill a Mockingbird* (1962)
Socialism – a set of beliefs that promote governmental ownership in order to promote a more equal distribution of resources among society. The ideology, like communism, limits exploitation and the class system.	*Sicko* (2007)

DON'T FORGET

Your job is to either identify some of these views in content you have studied or look at that content from the perspective of viewers with these views. Would the content be offensive or viewed differently by target audiences who held these beliefs (differential/preferred readings)?

ONLINE

Visit the Digital Zone for a case study of *The Crucible* – www.brightredbooks.net/subjects

THINGS TO DO AND THINK ABOUT

Choose one of the above ideologies and research it further. You could either create a presentation or, for more of a challenge, a persuasive essay. One or two examples of texts have been provided for you but do try to find your own.

This task may at first seem very challenging but if you break it down into the steps below, you should find it very straightforward. Your teacher may ask you to complete this task in a group.

Carefully consider any representations/stereotypes and then identify the use of technical or cultural codes, narrative devices (such as binary opposition or enigmas), the purpose of the text, the way in which it meets the needs of the audience and anything else relevant.

Structuring your argument (yes, this is considered an argument because you are persuading your audience that your chosen text supports or opposes certain ideologies):

- Firstly, introduce the text briefly, including a short synopsis and any themes it reveals.
- Secondly, introduce your chosen ideology and *briefly* explain some of the core beliefs. Include important theorists of the ideology.
- Continue by giving four or five clear examples from the content (such as language, narrative, representation) that support or oppose these beliefs. Do explain (identify/analyse/identify connotations/discuss) how that could lead to different readings of the text.

Finally, summarise (try to show conviction and a strong viewpoint) by briefly reflecting your own views on the subject.

ONLINE TEST

Head to the Digital Zone to test yourself on this topic.

REPRESENTATION
STEREOTYPES

HOW PEOPLE, PLACES AND EVENTS ARE PORTRAYED BY THE MEDIA

The word 'representation' literally means re-presentation. Even if certain events or portrayals appear at first to be realistic, remember that all the forms of media have been constructed intentionally, through a series of carefully considered decisions, for a particular effect. It is our job to try to work out what sort of *realities* are being presented, and why. Aspects of reality, such as people, places, time, events, communities, class, age, gender, sexuality, disability, race, ethnicity and cultures, are all presented to us from a particular perspective in order to create specific meaning within the text. Presenting events out of context, by editing or only showing partial truths in a certain way, will create an altered meaning (or spin).

How does it work?

Once upon a time, when we were very, very young, we were exposed to artificial versions of reality. Landscapes such as the 'deep, dark woods' presented in fairy tales such as 'Hansel and Gretel' and 'Little Red Riding Hood' were places to be feared. Princesses were good and beautiful and often played the victim; they needed a dashing Prince to save them and luckily there was usually one to hand. Witches were evil monstrous creatures who meant harm. You get the idea ...

Eventually, if repeated enough, presentations become stereotypes.

STEREOTYPES

The media is very powerful and has the ability to persuade. This can be very dangerous as stereotypes can be negative and sometimes even harmful to a group or individual. However, in the right context they help us understand character types and make meanings from texts. Stereotypes establish an image very quickly for the viewer or reader and are formed by grouping people together by shared characteristics – rather than by each individual's features or personalities. These are usually oversimplified and easily recognisable by the audience.

> **DON'T FORGET**
> Looking out for generalisations will help you recognise and analyse representations and stereotypes in your texts.

Mirror, mirror on the wall – who's the fairest of them all? And, by the way, who decides?

Consider poor Snow White (first written in 1937), despite being perilously close to death at the mercy of her evil stepmother, she managed to survive (thanks to the help of the Huntsman who took pity on her) only to arrive at the house of the seven dwarves who agreed to let her stay on the condition that she did all of the housework and cooking. Luckily, after a close shave with a poisoned apple, she was revived from death by her Prince.

contd

Representation – Stereotypes

 **ACTIVITY**

The representation of Snow White could be said to promote negative gender stereotypes. How? Notice that characters were often named by characteristics rather than being given traditional names.

The Bond film *Skyfall* is a good example of interesting and obvious representations. This is partly because the audience may already have clear expectations of characters in the film and in order to keep viewers interested the creators have subverted (or challenged) these stereotypes.

 **ACTIVITY**

Examine some of the representations in *Skyfall* (2012) and see if you can work out how they may differ from audience expectations. For example, the character M (played by Judi Dench), head of the British Secret Service, is traditionally a man's role. She is unusually older, as is Bond, and their insecurities centering on their own abilities is a theme that is explored throughout the film. Bond's physical and mental suitability is frequently called into question. When you have considered the characterisation you should ask yourself why director Sam Mendes may have wanted to challenge the audience of a Bond film. Consider the expectations placed upon him to surprise and wow the audience of this twenty-third Bond movie, which marked the golden anniversary of the franchise!

Character	Any Obvious Stereotypes	Language Codes Either Technical or Cultural that Help Portray the Stereotype	Any Ways in which the Director has Tried to Subvert (or challenge) the Stereotypes
JAMES BOND	Stubborn and strong willed, handsome, mysterious, bit of an action man, loves the thrill of the chase, thrives in dangerous situations, risk taker, dismissive of authority.	For example, Chiaroscuro lighting during opening sequence (as he creeps around the corridors on a mission) – reveals little of his features; we can only see half of his face and he appears enigmatic. The tense and iconic music in this scene also adds a sense of mystery. His tuxedo costume suggests sophistication ...	Yes, he shows a much more vulnerable side to him as doubts about his own mental and physical abilities cloud his judgement. He is older and there are moments of hesitation that we are not used to seeing from Bond.
M			
EVE			
SILVA			
SEVERINE			

You can do this for any text – it doesn't have to be a moving image.

 **ACTIVITY**

Consider, again, the example of 'Snow White'. What does the story suggest to us about the Evil Stepmother? We could say that Disney (the institution) is promoting the negative beliefs that step-parents are wicked. With a partner try to think of other examples of representations that support this view. To what extent do you think that this could be considered problematic? (Are all step-parents wicked?)

 THINGS TO DO AND THINK ABOUT

It is good practice to be aware of any representations being portrayed in any content you are studying. Try looking at a variety of moving images, news stories, print advertisements and film posters. The wider your exposure to different texts, the better prepared you will be for the exam. Consider representations of age, traditional gender roles, youth groups, refugees, the unemployed, the homeless, ethnicity and racial stereotyping. Try to come up with as many more as you can and add to your list as you come across them.

 ONLINE

For a more in-depth look at representations and stereotypes practice decoding as many as you can. Follow the link at www.brightredbooks.net/subjects for some examples.

 DON'T FORGET

To fully prepare for your exam you should consider both *how* and *why* representations have been created. Consider the technical, cultural and narrative codes, audience purpose and any institutional agendas. During the planning stage of your assignment, you should also consider the representations you are trying to create in your own work and remember that they shouldn't be there without clear justification.

 ONLINE

Go to the Digital Zone for a worksheet to help you plan your own representations – www.brightredbooks.net/subjects

 DON'T FORGET

It would show insight if, in response to your exam questions, you also considered which, if any, groups, places or events are being under-represented. For example, there is no shortage of the representation of disability in film, but it often appears as the focus of the main storyline and is far less evident in the supporting cast and background.

 ONLINE TEST

Test yourself on this topic at www.brightredbooks.net/subjects

25

NARRATIVE

NARRATIVE 1

OVERVIEW

Not all stories are as original as you think! When we are analysing a text it is useful to be able to recognise certain patterns hidden within the narrative. A recognisable structure helps us to make sense of the order of the information presented, and helps us identify key scenes or turning points in the plot.

At N5 level, it is expected that you will be able to use a number of different approaches to help you analyse complex media content in a sophisticated and thorough manner. Remember that you need this skill for *both* parts of the course. Once you have had a go at analysing texts and can begin to recognise structures, you will then be in a better position to apply these structures to your own media content. This section applies, on the whole, to moving image texts.

With a partner, take a moment to discuss the difference between a **story** and a **narrative**.

TODOROV

Tzvetan Todorov.

The narrative can often follow a pattern identified by Bulgarian philosopher, Tzvetan Todorov.

In a nutshell, Todorov recognised that film narrative exists as a process of cause and effect (a bit like our own lives) and categorised the stages as follows:

Equilibrium	Normality. Everything is calm. "Once upon a time in a land far away…"
Disruption	An interruption of that normality by a character or event.
Recognition	That disruption has taken place.
Repair	An attempt to repair the disruption.
New Equilibrium	A resolution and return to a new normality.

In order to help familiarise yourself with Todorov's narrative theory, study the example below, then try it out on a simple story that you a familiar with.

Equilibrium	Disruption	Recognition	Repair	New Equilibrium
Little Red Riding Hood sets off to see her Grandma.	Big Bad Wolf stalks her through woods.	Little Red Riding Hood notices Grandma looks very strange.	Hunter rescues Little Red Riding Hood and cuts open wolf to reveal an unharmed Grandma.	Everything goes back to normal and they all lived…

contd

Recognising Narrative Structure

It is harder to recognise this structure in a longer text. Not all films have *linear narratives*, meaning they are not always presented in the order in which they happen. Some stories use *flashbacks* (perhaps to reveal back-story), *subplots* (to create a more complex story), or different *viewpoints* (which place the audience with a certain character giving them an insight into their world).

 ACTIVITY

Can you think of examples of films that use these techniques? What was the purpose of using that particular narrative structure? Consider how you could have told the same story differently.

Sometimes switching between different characters can create fear and suspense in the audience as they know what is going to happen next, whereas the character doesn't. All of this can make it tricky to identify the different stages of narrative. It may help to first jot down the most important points of the *main storyline* on separate post-it notes, then try grouping them into the five stages. It is not an exact science so don't lose heart if it takes a while to get the hang of it. Get into the habit of filling in the template provided online as you watch new films/TV programmes or advertisements.

IDENTIFYING CHARACTER TYPE

Russian critic **Vladimir Propp** (1895–1970) identified a number of character roles common to most storylines, they are as follows:

Hero	Reacts to the donor and wins the princess.
Princess (and often her father)	The hero deserves her but she is often also sought after by the villain. Often marries the hero at the end of the story.
Villain	Struggles against the hero.
Donor or mentor	Prepares the hero or gives him some magical object.
Helper	Helps the hero in his quest.
False Hero	Takes credit for the heroes action and tries to win the princess.
Dispatcher	Sends hero off on his journey.

EXAMPLE:

In *Harry Potter and the Chamber of Secrets*, the characters fit quite well into Propp's theory:

The Villain – Lord Voldmort
The Hero – Harry Potter
The Donor – The Phoenix who provides tools such as a 'sorting hat'
The Helper – Ron Weasley or Hermione Granger
The Princess – Ginny Weasley (and her father, Arthur Weasley, and Dumbledore, who acts as a father figure)
The Dispatcher – Moaning Myrtle, helps show Harry the way
The False Hero – Professor Gilderoy Lockhart

THINGS TO DO AND THINK ABOUT

Not all texts have all characters and some will double up and fit into more than one category. Directors or **institutions** love to subvert the narrative (change our expectations of characters or plot): it keeps us watching.

Now try to list as many character types from films or stories you know well.

 ONLINE

For practice, download the **worksheet** at www.brightredbooks.net and use it for any texts that you are studying.

 DON'T FORGET

Remember you can do this to make your own stories more interesting.

 VIDEO LINK

Watch the clip at www.brightredbooks.net for a less predictable example of new equilibrium!

 DON'T FORGET

If you are planning your own short film or trailer etc, consider planning your characters using Propp's theory. Remember that this will satisfy the audience as they will recognise the narrative structure to one that is familiar to them. They expect it!

 DON'T FORGET

Remember, in media studies, you have think about narrative not in isolation, but consider the effect it has on context: both audience and institution.

 ONLINE TEST

Head to www.brightredbooks.net to test yourself on narrative.

NARRATIVE

NARRATIVE 2

STRUCTURES, CODES AND CONVENTIONS

As discussed in Narrative 1, narrative refers to the way that the different elements of the plot are organised. The content could be a TV drama where we would arrange characters, action and setting or a documentary, where we would use voice-overs, re-enactments (again character, actions and setting), facts and perhaps expert opinions by way of an interview. A print advert has a narrative in much the same way: pictures, layout, call to action and text, for example. Narrative structure refers to the way in which the key elements are constructed to create meaning. We have already looked at several recognisable structures recognised by Tzvetan Todorov and Vladimir Propp; now consider the following.

Lévi-Strauss and binary oppositions

French theorist Lévi-Strauss claimed in 1958 that plot was propelled through *binary oppositions*. This means that two elements (parts) of the story, or picture, have to oppose or contradict each other. This creates conflict. Some examples are given below. They work by creating conflict and therefore interest.

ACTIVITY

Complete the table (in your jotter) with any further examples of binary oppositions that you can think of and give examples from content that you know well.

Example of Binary Opposition Characteristic	
Good versus Evil (for example, any superhero film)	Freedom versus Slavery (for example, *Roots* (1977) or *12 Years a Slave* (2013))
Rich versus Poor (for example, *Trishna* (2011)/ *Slumdog Millionaire* (2008))	Predator versus Prey (for example, *Psycho* (1960))
Reality versus Fantasy (or Man versus Bear – for example, *Paddington* (2014))	Old versus Young (for example, Du Maurier's *Rebecca*)
Civilised versus Primitive	Strong versus Weak
Male versus Female	Peace versus War
First World versus Third World	Winners versus Losers
Working Class versus Middle Class	Love versus Hate
Man versus Nature	Friendship versus Betrayal

ENIGMA CODES AND ACTION CODES

Enigma codes and action codes both create suspense in the narrative. The first by unanswered questions, the second by anticipation of an action's resolution.

The hermeneutic code (enigma)

Leaves the audience guessing what is going to happen next. It creates unanswered questions and therefore mystery to draw the audience in.

> **EXAMPLE:**
>
> At the end of the film *Citizen Kane* by Orson Welles (1941) the audience is left wondering who or what *Rosebud* is. (Kane murmurs the word 'Rosebud' on his deathbed.) The film, which is much celebrated, was ahead of its years in terms of its unusual narrative. Soap writers often rely on enigmas in the form of cliffhangers at the end of an episode to hook the audience into watching the next episode. Often films with complex non-linear narrative structures (such as Tarantino's *Reservoir Dogs* (1992) or Scorsese's *Shutter Island* (2010)) work on enigma codes as the audience has to work hard to piece together the strands of the story in order to work it out.

DON'T FORGET

In your exam you may be asked to identify narrative structures, codes or conventions from a text you are familiar with but at National 5 level you will also be expected to go one step further, for example, to show how the audience may respond, as in 2017 SQA N5 exam.
For this particular question you could show an awareness of how certain binary oppositions are typical of a certain genre, for example, the hero and villain in a superhero film. Audiences would expect this.

contd

The proairetic code (action code)

Similar to the enigma codes, avoids revealing all of the facts and drops in clues to suggest what will happen next. They are significant events which move the narrative forward. Resolution is produced through action.

> **EXAMPLE:**
> The crime genre is a perfect place to look for action codes. Detective films often serve to solve a mystery that has been revealed at the beginning.

MORE CODES

Other codes recognised by Barthes are the semic code, the symbolic code and the cultural code.

The semic code

Present 'connotations' to us through **signs**. These could represent character, settings, reveal hidden meanings or clarify meanings.

The symbolic code

This is similar to the semantic code but creates new deeper or 'symbolic' meanings. Usually through contrasts or conflicts.

The cultural code

The cultural code refers to any element in a narrative that references common knowledge such as historical, mythological, societal, religious, cultural or scientific knowledge. An assumed (to be true) general knowledge about the world.

ACTIVITY

1. Can you think of any films that rely heavily on enigmas?
2. Can you think of examples of action codes?
3. Identify an example of a superhero/comic film such as *Spider-Man*.

You should make a detailed mind map of both the villain and the hero. Try to make it as detailed as possible.

Identify a Hero and a Villain (see Propp's character types on page 27 if you need help with this).

How are they portrayed to the audience so that you can identify the opposition? (Consider a range of cultural and technical codes the different points of characterisation: the way they act; the way other characters act around them; the way they speak/what they say; what others say about them, the way they look (costumes/make-up), whether or not they are represented by a change in tone/mood – perhaps through music or lighting or unusual camera angles; use of any obvious stereotypes; and so on.)

4. Consider carefully how these codes might help the audience understand the character and how that in turn helps them understand the narrative.

Now answer the following question in detail.

> a) Identify an example of a narrative code, convention or structure in media content you have studied. (You should explain the binary opposition and give the example clearly and concisely.)
>
> b) Show how your example helps the audience recognise the genre.

VIDEO LINK

You should further explore examples of Barthes' narrative codes to strengthen your knowledge of this topic. Use this as a starting point for further self-study – head to the Digital Zone to see some of the codes in action – www.brightredbooks.net/subjects

ONLINE TEST

Test your knowledge of this topic on the BrightRED Digital Zone!

THINGS TO DO AND THINK ABOUT

When you have answered Question 4, read through information on Barthes on the Digital Zone and complete the same question by using any examples of the five codes discussed.

NARRATIVE

NARRATIVE 3

TV DRAMA NARRATIVE

Although there are many similarities between narrative structures in TV drama and film, there are also some interesting differences.

We refer to film as 'short-form' storytelling and to long-running TV dramas as 'long-form' storytelling.

TV drama is often (but not always) created as a *series made up from a number of episodes. Long-form storytelling is usually made up* of continual storylines that flow from episode to episode.

A serial uses the same character leads but has a more continual storyline, whereas, traditionally, a series has the same leads but tends to have a more self-contained storyline with some sort of conclusion.

Depending on the length, each episode is likely to stand as a story in its own right. This is because, although it is part of a much bigger and more complex story, it has to be entertaining in its own right. Not every audience member will be aware of what went before or how events will impact future storylines; they may not be invested fans, but the makers of the content still want to engage all viewers.

Story arcs

Long-form storytelling often relies heavily on character development. Audience members often spend years with a character or characters.

An episode gives the illusion that the characters in the story exist in 'real time'. Between episodes an open story arc is a unique feature of long-form storytelling. This adds an extra layer of reality. Added to this, many of the storylines will centre on very real issues such as poverty, specific illnesses and relationship problems as well as some more light-hearted and often humorous issues.

A story arc can be introduced (much like the equilibrium of a film) and then developed over subsequent episodes. Think about your favourite character from a TV drama. What storylines have they been involved in and how did they develop and change as a result?

EPISODES AND SCENES – A CLOSER LOOK

Scene function was a notion originally introduced by French literary theorist Roland Barthes and later translated and explored further by Seymore Chapman.

An episode is made up of a number of scenes (a scene can generally be considered to consist of at least a couple of camera shots set within a particular setting and time). Of course, each scene should, like film, convey something important and contribute to the overall episode. It is common for more than one storyline to exist in one episode, adding complexity.

Key scenes and supporting scenes

Key scenes, sometimes called *kernel* scenes, generally convey the main progression of the story – that is, they move the story forward. They could explore a confrontation, obstacle, complication or disturbance – whatever its function it will be an integral part of the main story.

Supporting scenes, sometimes called **satellite scenes**, have entirely different functions, for example: to introduce a new character; for clarification and exposition (for example, explanation or description); to introduce a change in atmosphere and tone (ambience); to foreshadow or set up events to come; to provide a framework (context) for the main story; to operate as a solution to fill in potential gaps in the storyline for the audience;

contd

to provide continuity; or perhaps to provide a contrasting tone. Imagine kernels to be the skeleton of the episode and satellites to be the flesh.

Watch an episode from a TV drama with which you are familiar. Now select a number of scenes that you enjoyed and ask yourself the following questions:

1. Is this a key scene or a supporting scene (could the story be told without it)?
2. What do we learn in the scene?
3. What is its function?
4. Now decide how many storylines you can identify in your episode. Can you recognise any of the scene functions discussed above?
5. Would somebody who was not so familiar with the storylines know which were supporting scenes?
6. What difficulties might the novice viewer experience when watching the different types of scenes?

THE STRUCTURE OF A TV EPISODE

The diagram below should help you to understand the overall structure of a TV episode (according to the theory recognised by Barthes) and help you identify the typical structure of a TV episode.

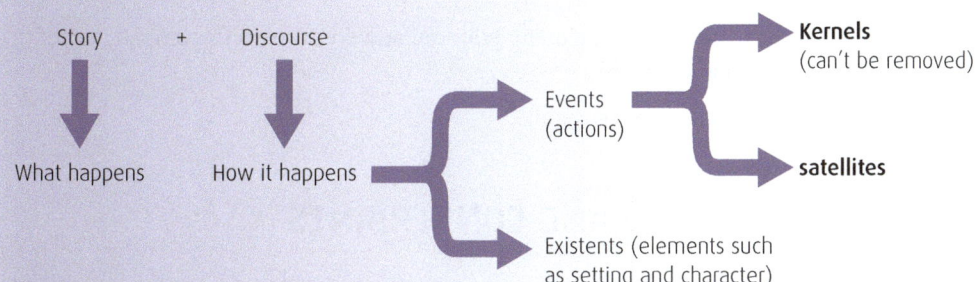

It is hoped that you can now see that TV is a complex form to get right as it has to work on so many different levels and across different time frames.

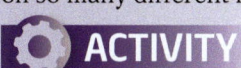

See if you can create a list of different storyline scenes to replace an episode of a TV drama that you are familiar with – for example, the final episode of *Game of Thrones* or *Friends*. You will first have to think of an impactful storyline or two. Think about the function of your scenes very carefully.

See if you can storyboard at least one kernel scene and one satellite scene – perhaps the opening or closing scenes?

THINGS TO DO AND THINK ABOUT

1. What roles could we argue long-form TV dramas play in society?

   Go online for ideas on how you might answer this in a 'role of the media' type question.

2. Research Internet discussions on the final series of *Game of Thrones*. How could these threads include the viewer to the extent of providing social interaction? Do you think these members of the audience feel a sense of belonging?

DON'T FORGET

Don't get hung up on the theory; the main thing to take from this chapter is that an episode is made up of different scenes, which, in turn, continue on to a long story arc in order to fulfil the requirements of a series and satisfy the audience.

ONLINE

Head to www.brightredbooks.net/subjects for extension comments on the Things To Do And Think About activity.

DON'T FORGET

The Things to Do and Think About activity is a real challenge – but it will encourage high-order thinking!

ONLINE TEST

Test your knowledge of Television Narrative on www.brightredbooks.net/subjects

INSTITUTIONS

INTERNAL CONSTRAINTS

WHAT IS AN INSTITUTION?

The term 'institution' in media goes beyond the traditional meaning of organisation. It refers to any organisation (or individual) who has an influence over the production of media content. This influence could be a set of ideals or an artistic vision or it could refer to regulations to which the producers must adhere. When we consider the context-based key aspect of 'institutions' at N5 we are asked to consider both 'internal and external controls and constraints' (the aspects from within or out-with the organisation that have any effect on the content or its distribution). To focus on this aspect is a reminder to us that we can't just look at the content as a product produced purely in the name of entertainment, but as a business. A number of other factors have shaped the final product before it reaches the target audience, and this is the focus of our interest for this section.

There are numerous institutional aspects – some obvious; some not. As well as looking at how the text has been made, we need to think about 'who' made the text and for what purpose, because this will most certainly have had an effect on the production process in one way or another.

Examples of constraints might be:

- External – legal, self-regulatory/codes of practice, market controls, societal controls or technological constraints
- Internal – financial, ownership including editorial and creative style, company (brief, mission statement and so forth)

Let's look at some of those in more detail.

INTERNAL CONTROLS AND CONSTRAINTS

Who made the content?

Ownership is one of the first considerations when looking at institutions. Media companies range in size from very small to large broadcasting companies such as the British Broadcasting Corporation (BBC), News Corp or Disney. Before you continue, think about who is behind the texts you are studying.

Disney is one of the most diverse and lucrative media corporations of the present day. They have to adhere to the expectations of their audience – this is a constraint. What would you expect from a Disney production? Consider values, typical narratives and character expectations.

DON'T FORGET

Don't forget to research the company or companies now if you haven't already done so.

Would it surprise you to discover that Disney also own Miramax, the company behind the film *Pulp Fiction* (1994)? So *Pulp Fiction* is a Disney production although the audience would not expect it to be so. Disney have a certain reputation for producing films with traditional family values and *Pulp Fiction* does not fit into this ideology – nor do *Trainspotting* (1996), *Gangs of New York* (2002) nor *Kill Bill: Volume 1* (2003), which are also Miramax films. It is for this reason that they have to maintain some distance. The promotion, distribution and marketing are just as important as the production and each production has to be very careful about how they do this.

The BBC Charter places constraints on the type of content they can produce. They are a public service, non-profit broadcaster, financed through the British television licence system. They have no political or financial control – they are expected to be non-biased in their broadcasting.

contd

Institutions – Internal constraints

ACTIVITY

Research and familiarise yourself with the BBC Charter and consider what limitations this could place on content they wish to produce.

One of the biggest constraints standing in the path of any producer will be *budget* and *funding*. The available budget will directly determine the finished content. Directors don't have 'free reign' with the budget – absolutely every penny has to be accounted for. The budget is a finite resource (this means it is limited)! All production crew, support services, actors, supporting artists, production, location and post-production services and so forth have to be budgeted for before anything else. So, for example, if certain specialist equipment or expertise is required for a particular effect, and the budget is not available, then alternatives have to be sought. All producers have to manage the budget and creatives such as directors have to find a way to work within those constraints.

A good example of a budgetary constraint can be found in connection to the film *Apocalypse Now* (1979). Director Francis Ford Coppola financed much of the film himself due to a catastrophic series of unfortunate events.

First, *casting*. Coppola wanted Steve McQueen for the part of Willard. He refused (as did Jack Nicholson, Robert Redford and Al Pacino). Harvey Keitel accepted but it became apparent as filming began that he was not suitable for the part. Eventually, he secured a much lesser known and more cost-effective actor – Martin Sheen. Other constraints that delayed the production significantly were the weather – a typhoon wiped out the entire set, which had to be rebuilt, having a massive impact on time and budget, and the health of the cast and crew – at one point Marlon Brando (who had arrived on set overweight and unprepared for the part) suffered a heart attack, although he did continue the shoot. To combat the issue of Marlon Brando's weight, Coppola decided to film his scenes entirely in the shadows, which ultimately added to his enigmatic characterisation. Sometimes a constraint can lead to positive outcomes!

VIDEO LINK

Watch a short video online to learn about the history of Walt Disney and some of the companies they now own at www.brightredbook.net/subjects

Act of Valor (2012), a film realistically depicting the operations of the military elite, negotiated budgetary constraints brilliantly as they used real Navy SEALs and live military operations within their film. This not only resulted in an exceptional sense of authenticity and realism but saved them millions of dollars. They used equipment such as a submarine, which was only above water for 45 minutes before submerging, and combined their filming schedule with pre-existing training missions. This saved them money and also resulted in the film being far more realistic and immersive than it would otherwise have been.

Many directors themselves are considered institutions in their own right. **Auteur theory** suggests that the director has overriding creative input. A certain director may carry with them certain personal ideologies or bring their own unique style to the filming of the production. The decisions they make will influence a production and is usually why they have been asked to be involved in the production in the first place. Such directors include Ken Loach, Alfred Hitchcock, Francis Ford Coppola, Danny Boyle, Woody Allen, Christopher Nolan and Roman Polanski.

DON'T FORGET

You will have to write about the internal constraints that you had to deal with during the creation or production of your assignment. Avoid turning this into a rant about a lack of equipment and budget; although this clearly affects your content, the idea is too simplistic. The examiner would be more interested to hear how you creatively dealt with those constraints. These are authentic and considered planning decisions.

THINGS TO DO AND THINK ABOUT

Make a list of all of the possible internal constraints that creators of content could face and consider how those issues could affect the production of a short film, a TV advert and a film poster.

ONLINE TEST

Test your knowledge of institutional constraints on the Digital Zone.

INSTITUTIONS
EXTERNAL CONSTRAINTS

TARGET AUDIENCE

The audience themselves are one of the biggest examples of external constraints. Productions are constrained by the target audience and their expectations. They have to appeal to the audience in a novel and entertaining way, yet still stay within the boundaries of the expectations of, for example, the genre. A director may want to push the boundaries of genre expectations or break traditions altogether – this would be a huge gamble and often the reason why media companies and their artistic creators clash! Distribution times may also be a constraint; for example, it may be preferable to release horror films around Halloween for additional impact and hype.

RULES AND REGULATIONS

Rules and regulations regulating the media industry present another set of constraints. The industry places strict guidelines on working conditions for crew members and such like (as does the Actors' Equity Association – the union for actors and supporting actors – and the union BECTU (Broadcasting, Entertainment, Communications and Theatre Union)).

There are many different regulations and codes to consider if you want to film in public spaces, private or council property and if you want to use children or animals in your production. (Child protection regulations require that everybody on set has a criminal disclosure certificate if anyone on set is aged 16 or under.)

The main ones to consider (although there are more) are:

- British Board of Film Classification (BBFC) – age certification
- Advertising Standards Authority (ASA)
- Committee of Advertising Practice (CAP)
- Intellectual Property Office (IPO)
- Independent Press Standards Organisation (IPSO)

 ACTIVITY

Find an example of a production of any description and make a list of all of the constraints they encountered and show how they overcame them. You will find some very useful information on the IMBD website: www.imdb.com

When analysing content, you should always consider how any constraints have influenced the final content as this will undoubtedly have resulted in a number of planning decisions. Constraints shape content.

ONLINE

Follow the links on the Digital Zone www.brightredbooks.net/subjects to the agencies listed here to learn more about each.

DON'T FORGET

If you are producing content of any description for your assignment you must make sure you adhere to the regulations. This is sometimes a hard thing to do – especially if you are set on specific ideas that work well artistically. However, like any producer, you must. Use the task opposite to help you work out how you might regulate your own content and ideas. Show that you can be creative and can problem solve.

Institutions – External constraints

THINGS TO DO AND THINK ABOUT

Look at the storyboard below very carefully.

1

2

3

Now let us imagine that this was for a 12 certificate. Identify which regulation has been broken then re-plan the storyboards making sure that you engage the older audience while following the regulations for a certificate 12. The regulations have been listed here to help you.

Here are the key guidelines from the BBFC for age 12 suitability. These are your guidelines.

12A/12 – Suitable for 12 years and over

Discrimination
Discriminatory language or behaviour must not be endorsed by the work as a whole. Aggressive discriminatory language or behaviour is unlikely to be acceptable unless clearly condemned.

Drugs
Misuse of drugs must be infrequent and should not be glamorised or give instructional detail.

Imitable behaviour
No promotion of potentially dangerous behaviour which children are likely to copy. No glamorisation of realistic or easily accessible weapons such as knives. No endorsement of anti-social behaviour.

Language
There may be moderate language. Strong language may be permitted, depending on the manner in which it is used, who is using the language, its frequency within the work as a whole and any special contextual justification.

Nudity
There may be nudity, but in a sexual context it must be brief and discreet.

Sex
Sexual activity may be briefly and discreetly portrayed. Moderate sex references are permitted, but frequent crude references are unlikely to be acceptable.

Threat
There may be moderate physical and psychological threat and horror sequences. Although some scenes may be disturbing, the overall tone should not be. Horror sequences should not be frequent or sustained.

Violence
There may be moderate violence but it should not dwell on detail. There should be no emphasis on injuries or blood, but occasional gory moments may be permitted if justified by the context. Sexual violence may only be implied or briefly and discreetly indicated, and its depiction must be justified by context.

This is a challenge – you are being asked to widen the audience appeal but not disappoint an older audience with expectations from the genre. First, list all the issues with each sequence as it stands, and then list the regulations that it breaches in its current state; now be very creative and come up with solutions.

ONLINE

Visit the links listed on the Digital Zone for further information/downloads from the BBFC.

ONLINE TEST

Test your knowledge of institutional constraints on the Digital Zone – www.brightredbooks.net/subjects

INSTITUTIONS

ADVERTISING REGULATIONS

A CLOSER LOOK AT ADVERTISING AND REGULATION

The advertising industry works hard to create effective adverts while ensuring that the content meets the guidelines set out by the regulating bodies.

The Advertising Standards Agency (ASA) is the independent body responsible for regulating the UK advertising industry. It is their job to make sure that all advertisers act responsibly by complying with the agreed guidelines.

The Committee of Advertising Practice (CAP) works in association with the ASA and it is their job to write the advertising codes.

There are two main guides, Broadcast and Non-Broadcast, and each are divided into categories: alcohol, gambling, food and soft drinks, health and beauty, and tobacco.

Different regulations apply specifically to each category; however, the message is the same: adverts should be: '*legal, decent, honest and truthful*' and should not '*mislead, harm or offend and be socially responsible*' (ASA:2018).

ACTIVITY

1. Visit the CAP website (www.cap.org.uk) and find out the four main rules governing advertising and children.
2. Find one example of a case relating to children or young people and advertising and answer the questions below.

What was the Name of the Advert or Campaign and Who Were Their Creators?	What were the Main Issues or Complaints?	Were the Complaints Upheld?	Do You Agree with the Decision and Why?

ACTIVITY

Believe it or not, the advert below was once considered perfectly acceptable.

See if you can find further examples of print adverts that were around before the ASA and CAP regulations were put in place (in 1961). How many would be in breach of the rules by today's standards and in what way?

ONLINE

Find out more by following the link on the Digital Zone to the ASA website – www.brightredbooks.net/subjects

DON'T FORGET

Advertisers cannot possibly please everyone. All of the adverts mentioned here are creative, original and clever and effectively received by the majority of their target audience.

DON'T FORGET

As we discuss further in the 'audience' section, different audiences read a text depending on their own values and experiences of life. If a complaint is raised, it has to be investigated. This makes the creative process very challenging. As we know, societal views change all the time, and what was once considered distasteful could become completely acceptable.

ONLINE

You can access the full report by following the link in the Digital Zone.

Institutions – Advertising regulations

GENDER STEREOTYPING: DEPICTIONS, PERCEPTIONS AND HARM

The role of gender stereotyping in advertising is another very interesting area for us to consider.

On 18 July 2017, the ASA published a report on gender stereotyping called: 'Depictions, Perceptions and Harm'. They found that *'[h]armful stereotypes can restrict choices, aspirations and opportunities of children, young people and adults'* and found the following to be unacceptable:

1 'Depicting family members creating a mess while a woman has sole responsibility for clearing it up'.
2 'Suggesting a specific activity is inappropriate for boys because it is stereotypically associated with girls, or vice versa'.
3 'Featuring a man trying and failing to undertake simple parental or household tasks'.
(*The Depictions, Perceptions and Harm Report*: ASA)

 **ACTIVITY**

Visit an adverting agency website and view some of their adverts. Identify campaigns that have both challenged and exploited gender stereotyping. You can use this task to help prepare yourself for the exam. Which ones do you think work best and why? You should always consider both the preferred reading and differential decoding. An example has been given to help you.

 ONLINE

Visit www.brightredbooks.net/subjects for an additional activity connected to this topic.

Name of Agency and the Campaign you Have Selected	GAP advert suggesting the boy would grow up to be academic and the girl a 'social butterfly'.
Preferred Reading. (How Could the Representations be Considered Effective?)	GAP clothing sells clothes that both girls and boys (or parents) may love.
Differential Decoding. (Could the Representations be Considered Problematic or Offensive to Some Audience Members?)	Some viewers complained that the advert suggested that girls were less likely to be as academically successful when they grew up. *The advert was subsequently removed by the clothing chain, so no further action was taken by the ASA.*
Have Gender Stereotypes Been Exploited or Challenged and How?	Exploited. It is still the case that there is a gender pay gap in society. Does this image reinforce the negative ideology that girls are less likely to be successful in their careers?
How is the Advert Effective in Meeting the Needs of the Campaign?	It shows the range of child's clothing available. The children look stylish, which reflects the brand.
How Does It Meet the Needs of the Audience?	It does show the range of clothing available. The children are both cute and look very sweet in the clothes selected. Many audience members would warm to this advert.

The ASA note that a lack of diversity would not be good for our society and that brilliant adverts come from challenging gender stereotypes.

 **ACTIVITY**

Try to create an idea for an advert for each of the following products. Your brief is to challenge the gender stereotypes!
- A washing powder advert
- An advert for a sports car
- An advert promoting a vacuum cleaner
- An advert for a lawnmower

 THINGS TO DO AND THINK ABOUT

As well as being very interesting to anyone studying media, the ASA and CAP websites should be your first port of call when you are researching any *external institutional constraints* for adverts you may want to create for your assignment or explore for the question paper.

 ONLINE TEST

Test yourself on this topic on the Digital Zone.

NEWS CONTENT AND THE ROLE OF THE MEDIA

NEWSPAPER FORMATS

WHAT IS NEWS?

The term 'news' refers to any current event and is a global media industry. Traditionally only shared via a traditional newspaper, it is now accessed on a number of online platforms as well as through TV news programmes. Regardless of consumer preference over their 'medium' of choice, the style of the content (and thus the meaning) differs considerably between publications (or channels).

TYPES OF NEWSPAPERS

> **DON'T FORGET**
>
> As a pupil of media, it is important that you both keep abreast of current affairs and also make yourself aware of varying styles, content, newsgroups (and who controls them) and the potential implications of ownership on the choice of stories published. There are resources at the end of this chapter for you to continue with your research into news media.

There are lots of different types of newspapers in the UK, for example: free newspapers, community newspapers, specialist newspapers, national daily newspapers and Sunday Newspapers – each, because of the content and style they choose, target a certain political or social group (see target audience page 82). National daily newspapers are typically classified as follows.

Broadsheets

Named as such because they were traditionally large in size (many have now downscaled), they are considered by most to be an 'up-market' or quality newspaper – both intelligent and 'respectable'. Typical subject matter includes debates on current national and international affairs as well as arts and culture. The subject matter is most likely to be serious, and reporting style less about journalistic opinion and based more on facts. **Broadsheet newspapers** favour a more *objective* approach to journalism (meaning their reporting style is more neutral or unbiased), employ a sophisticated and intelligent vocabulary and use evidence in the form of quotations from experts. The articles will be text led – longer with less of the paper given over to pictures – and the tone will often be formal.

Titles include: *The Times, The Independent* (now online only), *The Telegraph, The Guardian* and international business newspapers like *The Financial Times*.

contd

Mid-market tabloids

Mid-market tabloids balance serious reporting with human-interest pieces such as crime reporting and gossip items. As the name suggests they pitch themselves somewhere between tabloid and broadsheet style of journalism and titles. The *Daily Mail* and the *Daily Express* are mid-market tabloids distinguishable by their black *mastheads*.

Red-tops

Red-tops or tabloids are traditionally presented in a smaller format and the target audience tends (although not always) to lean towards the lower-middle and working classes. Subject matter is less serious and regularly reports on celebrity 'news', gossip, scandal and sport. They are often *sensationalist* in style (which means they use exaggeration to attract and entertain their target audience). They are image led (more emphasis on photographs) and employ *screaming headlines* and *puns* to catch attention. The style is informal, chatty and more *subjective* (or *biased*). Stories are usually confined to the UK (**demographic**). While still bound by the regulatory body *IPSO* – the *Independent Press Standards Organisation* – (and thus obliged to adhere to strict codes of practice), they will often find an angle that is entertaining and put their own *spin* on the story. This is why red-tops are often considered less reliable and frequently involved in legal proceedings!

 ACTIVITY

Find a news story that has been covered by both a broadsheet and a tabloid paper and draw comparisons. Remember that this is where English and media differ because as well as the content, you will be expected to reflect upon the context (especially the influence of institutions).

 **DON'T FORGET**

It is important that you understand the differences between broadsheet and tabloid newspaper formats and can recognise their typical selection of subject matter and style of journalism.

 THINGS TO DO AND THINK ABOUT

Find a story covered by both a broadsheet and a tabloid and do a more detailed analysis. Use the following to guide you in the right direction.

It would be excellent preparation for both your exam and Higher Media Studies if you closely examined wider coverage of a notable campaign, issue, scandal or event. This will give you plenty to analyse both in terms of content and context.

You should consider:

- the way the story has been presented or framed by the publication
- the style, including any form-specific codes that have been employed
- the purpose of the article(s)
- the ownership of the newspaper (you will have to research this – see the next chapter), including any hidden agendas you may identify
- the ways in which the content has influenced the audience either intentionally or unintentionally (consider **moral panic**).

These types of case studies often serve candidates of media studies well and much has been written about prolific news coverage, which means you will be able to research what others have written about them. Do make sure you form your own opinions. Choose something you are interested in and be prepared to do your research. These are big questions!

 DON'T FORGET

In order for you to recognise and analyse news articles effectively, you will have to be reading them on a regular basis! Active reading is much more effective – to do this you should make organised notes, for example, content and style and any audience reactions.

NEWS CONTENT AND THE ROLE OF THE MEDIA
PRESS OWNERSHIP, CIRCULATION, REGULATION AND FAKE NEWS

WHAT IS A 'FREE PRESS'?

In Britain we have a 'free press' system, which means the content of our press is not dictated by the government like in some countries; *however*, we have to be very aware of the ownership status of the press and the typical political loyalties of each because they will influence the content. (Remember they all have a very specific target audience and tend to lean one way or the other politically and as such in their coverage of stories.) Owners or senior editors act as **gatekeepers**; in other words, they decide if a story is newsworthy or not.

A long-standing question is whether the opinions published in the press are a reflection of their readers, or whether they influence their readers to adopt those opinions.

Websites like Newsworks can provide you with readership figures or a market overview that show a selection of circulation figures for the UK newspaper and online news market. The circulation figures should show you how much influence and power the press has in this country.

OWNERSHIP, POLITICAL BIAS AND AGENDA SELECTION OF NEWS

At the time of researching, just a few companies (Rupert Murdoch's News Corp UK and Lord Rothermere's Daily Mail Group) own, between them, a total of about 71 per cent of national newspapers, and just five companies control 80 per cent of news consumption if you include online platforms. If we can assume that the content does influence the readers and the political views of the owners are reflected in the content, we can easily understand how potentially problematic these influences can be on society. What issues might this cause? Consider whether the readers might start acting upon what it is that they are reading in the press, which may have been published for that very reason – to influence.

PRESS REGULATION AND FAKE NEWS

So, who regulates the press? The Independent Press Standards Organisation (IPSO) 'protect[s] people's rights, upholds high standards of journalism and helps to maintain freedom of expression'. Below are several of the key IPSO statements from the Editors' Code of Practice.

DON'T FORGET

There is a difference between circulation and readership. The former refers to how many copies are actually distributed (data can be found through ABC (the Audit Bureau of Circulations)); however, in any one household it may be that more than one person reads the same paper (readership). This is harder to monitor and relies more on the demographic profile of individuals (see the chapter on 'audience' PTK).

Visit the IPSO website yourself and research cases of complaints and the full version of the Code of Practice. A link can be found on the Digital Zone.

> The press must take care not to publish inaccurate, misleading or distorted information or images, including headlines not supported by the text.
> i) Everyone is entitled to respect for his or her private and family life, home, health and correspondence, including digital communications.
> ii) Journalists must not engage in intimidation, harassment or persistent pursuit.
> iii) In cases involving personal grief or shock, enquiries and approaches must be made with sympathy and discretion and publication handled sensitively. These provisions should not restrict the right to report legal proceedings.
> iv) All pupils should be free to complete their time at school without unnecessary intrusion.

contd

News content and the role of the media – Press ownership, circulation, regulation and fake news

v) Relatives or friends of persons convicted or accused of crime should not generally be identified without their consent, unless they are genuinely relevant to the story.

vi) The press must not seek to obtain or publish material acquired by using hidden cameras or clandestine listening devices; or by intercepting private or mobile telephone calls, messages or emails; or by the unauthorised removal of documents or photographs; or by accessing digitally-held information without consent (IPSO).

ACTIVITY

- Can you think of any current or past news stories where reports may have been in breach/or near breach of the above rules?
- Are there ways that journalists could evade (avoid) the above regulations while still upholding the rules – are there ways around them?

ONLINE TEST

Test your knowledge on the BrightRED Digital Zone – www.brightredbooks.net/subjects!

FAKE NEWS

We have learned that news content and style can differ greatly depending on type of newspaper, style, target audience and ownership. However, all of the newspapers mentioned are regulated.

Content produced for social media platforms such as Twitter, Vine, Facebook and Instagram is almost impossible to control because they are not subject to the same rigorous controls and, in recent times, the power of these platforms with their unregulated content reaching the masses on a scale never seen before has fuelled the idea of 'fake news'. More and more companies and institutions and individuals are pushing the boundaries of traditional marketing methods. Why do you think they would they want content to go viral?

There are a number of common types of fake news, varying in degrees of deception, such as a mismatch whereby the content connects two unrelated stories through the language of news, so a headline with a completely unrelated picture suggesting false connotations and fake news sites claiming to be legitimate and often bearing an uncanny resemblance to a real news site such as CNN. Some fake news is created for satire purposes (to entertain); **parodies**/spoofs are a common form of Internet entertainment and some people believe them as truth. Some stories are simply manipulated to create a different angle. Finally, some 'news' is completely fabricated.

Some people believe that sites such as Facebook screen content so that they are promoting only that which they support, thus limiting the spread of content they don't want. They call this a 'filter bubble'.

ACTIVITY

Research

What is '*clickbait*' and how does it work? How does it relate to 'fake news'?

For extra practice, look at fake news marketing campaigns for films such as *A Cure for Wellness* (2016) and *Watchmen* (2009).

THINGS TO DO AND THINK ABOUT

1 Research the owners (and their political loyalties) of the main UK tabloid and broadsheet newspapers. Head to the Digital Zone for a useful link to start you off.

2 Can you find and compare the style and tone of articles on the following topics as covered by both a broadsheet and a tabloid?

- The War on Terror
- Tax
- Immigration
- Brexit

NEWS CONTENT AND THE ROLE OF THE MEDIA

MEETING NEEDS AND ACHIEVING PARTICULAR PURPOSES

THE ROLE OF THE MEDIA

All media content has a role to play – nothing is created without purpose. At National 5, you will be expected to consider and explore the 'Role of the Media'. The roles of the media are wide and varied so you should never be limited in material for your answers. It is useful to remember not to see the role of the media as a new topic; much of this information will be familiar to you.

The main approaches to the role of the media (in media studies) are as follows:

- Meeting needs: education, information and entertainment
- Achieving particular purposes: profit, public service, promotion
- Influencing attitudes: intentionally or unintentionally

You could be asked to discuss any of the above, and so you will need a range of suitable texts to choose from.

MEETING NEEDS

ACTIVITY

Think about all the different reasons people have for consuming media content and consider why you consume the content that you do. How do audiences use media texts? Here are some ideas to start you off. Add to this list by considering all of the texts you have studied so far – try to give a variety of examples.

Reasons	Examples of Texts
For information	
For entertainment	
For education	
For Public Service	

To help us to better understand the role of the media in meeting audience needs, it is useful to look at some theoretical ideas. You can use these to back up your answers and support your evidence in your exam. You do not have to discuss theories, but it may add weight to your answer and help make your arguments clearer. There isn't enough room to explore all possible theories, so suggestions have been made for further research and it is highly recommended that you do undertake this research. Once we are familiar with some of the theory, we can use this information to help us understand how producers of media content use this information to appeal to the audiences.

Maslow's hierarchy of needs theory shown here was developed in 1943 by Abraham Harold Maslow. It counts humans needs beginning with our very basic human needs and builds to self-actualisation.

Self-actualisation – morality, creativity, lack of prejudice, acceptance of facts, problem solving.
Esteem – self esteem, confidence, achievement, respect of others, respect by others.
Love/Belonging – Friendship, family, intimacy
Safety – security, resources, family, health, etc.
Physiological – food, water, sleep and other bodily functions

contd

Can you see how some media content might fulfil some of our needs? For example, themes in films or other media may involve a sense of belonging or love or achievement and this can help motivate the audience.

ACTIVITY

Think of as many examples as you can for each level. The first has been done for you (think about social media usage as well).

1 Physiological needs

Cast Away (2000) is a survival film directed by Robert Zemeckis, starring Tom Hanks. The film follows the survival of the main character as he is marooned on a tropical island. He struggles for food, water and shelter to survive.

Man vs Wild – Bear Grylls shows the nation how to survive in the wild.

2 Safety   –
3 Love and belonging –
4 Esteem   –
5 Self-actualisation   –

Uses and Gratifications Theory (UGT) refers to mass communication and assumes the audience is active in their choices of media consumption. The potential uses can generally be grouped into five categories.

Audiences want:

- to be informed or educated
- to identify with the characters or situation in the narrative
- simple entertainment
- to enhance their social interactions
- escapism.

Audiences expect more and more from media content as social media pushes the boundaries, for example, audiences of *The Voice UK* will regularly see judge Will.I.Am filming his acts and tweeting. #thevoiceuk… This allows members of the audience to interact with the Twitter feed and become far more involved in the process than they ever would have before.

Can you think of any other TV shows that involve the audience?

ACHIEVING PARTICULAR PURPOSES

As mentioned above, much media content is created to achieve a profit for the creating institution. It can be easy to forget that when we look at the news headlines on a newspaper. News is business (see News section page 12).

THINGS TO DO AND THINK ABOUT

1. List all the media content that you know to be made for profit.
2. Some content is created with the intention of promotion (of people, ideas or organisations) and if content doesn't only have a profit motive but appears to be of benefit to society, it is likely to be a 'public service' production. Campaigns such as the Scottish government's drugs and alcohol awareness films and the Unilever's Dove 'real beauty' campaign fit into this category. Can you think of others?

DON'T FORGET

There will probably be more than one role of the media that you can identify. For example, the main purpose may be for profit, but to fulfil that role the content also has to entertain. If it doesn't entertain, nobody will want to see it and it won't bring in a profit.

ONLINE

Head to the Digital Zone to read an article from *Encyclopædia Britannica* on the definition of 'infotainment' – www.brightredbooks.net/subjects

ONLINE TEST

Test yourself on this topic at www.brightredbooks.net/subjects

NEWS CONTENT AND THE ROLE OF THE MEDIA
INFLUENCING ATTITUDES AND BEHAVIOURS

All content is capable of *influencing attitudes and behaviour either intentionally or unintentionally*. It is important to remember that different audiences will have different reactions to the content (see section on audience on page 52).

PREFERRED READING AND DIFFERENTIAL DECODING

According to cultural theorist Stuart Hall's theory, for a preferred reading to occur, the audience reads the text the way the author intended. But a differential decoding is always possible as some audience members hold different beliefs, experience or values (or subscribe to differing ideologies). This will result in an 'oppositional reading'. (It is also possible for an audience to partly accept the preferred reading (this is called a negotiated reading).) Consider the following:

A typical teen's fashion magazine may subscribe to the following ideologies (evident by the front cover).
- Looking good is essential.
- Losing weight is important.
- Fashion brands are significant.
- Celebrity culture is interesting.

An oppositional reading of these suggestions may believe the following.
- Looks are insignificant.
- Being healthy is more important than weight.
- Quality of clothing is more important than style.
- Celebrity culture is uninteresting.

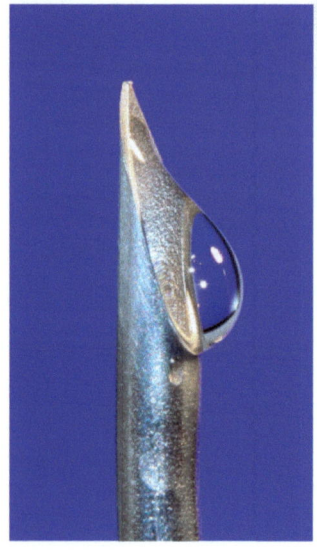

MORE THEORY!

The *Hypodermic Needle Model (sometimes called the Magic Bullet Theory)*, dating from the 1920s, suggests that information is passed directly from the text to the audience, on mass. It implies that we are extremely easily influenced and is now considered a little outdated and simplistic. It is what we refer to when we hear of a *'moral panic'*. The argument that violent video games in turn cause individuals to become violent puts this theory into practice.

The Two-Step Flow is a more updated theory, which suggests that the media has less power and audiences are less passive.

A less extreme theory of audience reception is the *Agenda Setting Theory*, which suggests that in order for an issue to be widely debated, discussed or actioned by the public it has to first enjoy extensive media coverage. In other words, the media 'set the agenda: the public act upon it'. According to Dearing and Rogers (1996) smoking was once limited to a personal issue before media intervened to make it a wider public health issue.

Some public service campaigns intentionally aim to influence the audience. Many have an extremely important role to play and many are extremely successful. Prostate Cancer UK (which is a charity partner of The Football League) run by Public Zone UK used its connection to raise awareness of the disease. There was a huge increase in traffic to the prostate cancer awareness website in the first week of the campaign. Awareness has continued to rise.

Some content will achieve more than one purpose or meet different needs.

ACTIVITY

1. Watch the videos on the Digital Zone and consider which role or roles of the media you think each fulfils and why.
2. What are the preferred readings?
3. How are they created?
4. Are there any possible differential readings?
5. Can you associate any potential problems with these readings?
6. Could you tie in any of the theories?

VIDEO LINK

Head to www.brightredbooks.net/subjects to watch the videos for this activity.

EXAMPLE OF A NATIONAL 5 QUESTION

Look at this role of the media style question below:

> Explain how media content you have studied meets the needs of the audience by entertaining. 10 marks.

You are expected to show, clearly, how aspects of your content have been constructed to entertain the audience. SQA ask that you show 'cause and effect' (which means the relationship between them). Tackle this by explaining a number of straightforward points or you can develop your points. You will be awarded one extra mark for each point of development or for the introduction of a new point. There is a maximum of 10 marks.

EXAMPLE:

According to The Uses and Gratifications Theory, an audience actively seeks to be entertained. The 2012 Bond film *Skyfall* directed by Sam Mendes entertains the audience in a number of ways.

First, by employing a range of cultural and technical codes. The orchestral music used in the opening scene is instantly recognisable as the Bond theme tune – fans of the film will be expecting this, and it helps provide a dramatic and entertaining opening to the film. (1 mark) The music continues to rise to a crescendo step by step as the opening scene progresses and this makes the audience feel tense fearing for Bond's safety. The music acts as a non-diegetic metaphor for danger keeping the audience on the edge of their seats. (1 mark for development of this point) Traditionally, the big Bond ballad would come at the opening of the film, but Mendes introduces the powerful song, by Adele, following the scene where Bond has been shot. The tense moment is followed by silence and it is at that point that the ballad begins in order to maximise the impact – the audience listen to the nostalgic song as Bond fights for his life. (1 mark)

Lighting is also used to add a sense of mystery to the film and the character of Bond. Our first shot of Bond is as a silhouette figure. (1 mark) As Bond approaches the camera only half of his face is lit. This chiaroscuro lighting effect introduces Bond as an enigmatic character – he looks mysterious and as if he is in danger, another expectation of a Bond film. (1 mark)

You would need five more points for full marks, and in the case of *Skyfall* you could discuss the typical genre expectations of a Bond film, the fast-paced editing used in the car and bike chases, the fight scene on top of the train or the relationships between M and Bond, Moneypenny and Bond and Eve and Bond. You could also extend your answer by further exploring the stages of UGT or Maslow's Hierarchy of needs. It is important to make clear that the examples you pick illustrate how the film is meeting the need for entertainment.

ACTIVITY

Complete the 2017 question for a text of your choice. Be aware of where you will be awarded marks, making sure that you do enough for 10 marks. Remember the instruction is to give a 'detailed response'.

THINGS TO DO AND THINK ABOUT

Research content to find one of the topics below and consider:
- What potential issues arise from the way the topic has been represented?
- What roles of the media can be identified in the content you have chosen?
- How are the key aspects used to represent an ideology?
- How could you apply at least two audience reception models to your media content?
- The use of social media by young people.
- The representation of 'beauty'.
- Gender, or age, stereotyping.
- Representations of social class.

ONLINE TEST

Test yourself on this topic at www.brightredbooks.net/subjects

NEWS CONTENT AND THE ROLE OF THE MEDIA

NON-FICTION FILMS AND PUBLIC INFORMATION FILMS

NON-FICTION TEXTS

There are many purposes of non-fiction texts and they may set out to explain or inform, persuade, recount, entertain or discuss. The texts vary enormously and included under this broad heading are those such as advertising, documentaries, reality TV, newspapers and public information films. Production content asked to consider in a Role of the Media question is the 'public information film'. This chapter will focus on the information film form.

VIDEO LINK
Watch *Life without Limits* on the Digital Zone.

ACTIVITY

Take a moment to complete the following tasks either in a group or individually.

- Make a list of as many different information or documentary films or TV programmes that you can think of.
- What do you think is the main purpose of each? Can you identify any secondary purposes?
- Based on your own research, who are the most prolific documentary film makers both past and present and what examples of their work have earned them that accolade?

If you do this exercise thoroughly it will give you some good examples to work with should this type of question appear in your exam.

Key questions to ask yourself.

When analysing a non-fiction film, you should consider the following:

- Is the film telling the complete truth? Is any information missing?
- How much is fact and how much is fiction and how do you know?
- How much of the creator's influence, values or beliefs are apparent in the text and is it hidden, obvious or both?

ACTIVITY

Stories Lived is a non-profit website and film festival showcasing true stories through the medium of moving image. *Life without Limits* is a short film by writer, director and producer Blaise Borrer. Told from first-person perspective, the film explores popular beliefs about autism spectrum disorder. Watch it a couple of times on the Digital Zone and answer the following questions:

1. What do we know to be fact and what could be fiction?
2. Is Borrer (the creator) biased? If so, give clear examples of where in the film bias is strongest.
3. What key aspects have been used to convey his message? Think of the way the story is narrated. Consider the narrative structure and any representations or form-specific codes such as lighting, music and recognisable camera shots or sequences.
4. What is the main purpose of the film (think about the preferred reading from page 44)? Could there be any differential readings from certain audience members? Give examples.
5. Is the film getting the message across? Are there parts that aren't effective?

Once you have completed this activity you should pick several other examples of the many films on the site and complete the same task while considering the question below.

Do any of these convey what we could consider a non-biased truth? If not, why not and give examples to back up your opinion.

DON'T FORGET
These films are excellent inspiration for generating ideas you could use for your own assignment. If yours is good enough you could consider entering it onto the Stories Lived Website. Films must be no more than five minutes long and entry details are on the website.

PUBLIC INFORMATION FILMS

Some films are made (usually through government funding) in order to address a problem or issue in society. These are called public information films. Typical topics could be addressing drink driving, drug abuse, the harmful effects of smoking and other health-related issues.

Typical conventions to look out for in this type of film are:

1. *Commentary* often in the form of voice-overs. This enables the story to be told in the way they intended.
2. *The voice of 'experts'* (they may or may not be academic experts but are there to act as an authority on the subject). This gives the subject credibility.
3. *Observational, (fly on the wall) or use of embed reporters during filming.* This allows us to observe the subjects in their natural habitat. Be careful with this one – the clips may be re-enactments, carefully edited or conditions set up to predict a probable outcome. None of this is pure observation.
4. *Recount* – a personal experience.
5. As above, *dramatised (or scripted) scenes* to reinforce perspective and persuade the audience to subscribe to their point of view.
6. Snappy and memorable *catchphrases* such as 'STOP' 'THINK!'

In order for a creator (such as the government) to get their message across, they have to meet the needs of the audience – this should be a very familiar concept to you by now.

Try to put yourself in the shoes of the filmmaker – it would be very hard to produce a really hard-hitting public information film without being creative. So this is something we accept.

As a National 5 student you should be able to demonstrate: how much of the film is pure information by giving examples and how much there is to entertain – again by identifying those elements of the film.

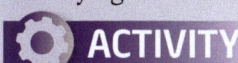

Try this now with a public information film of your choice. You should watch it a couple of times and see if you can identify the elements above. Look out for key aspects, such as representation or language codes, that have been used especially in any re-enactment scenes.

Then and Now

A useful and interesting exercise is to compare a traditional early public information film with a current production. This shows you how the needs of the audience have changed over the years. Most would consider the simple 'explanation heavy' style of storytelling boring and would most likely switch off. As moving image becomes more and more sophisticated so do our tastes. Most of these types of films rely on a combination of showing us and telling us – the showing reinforces what the narrator is telling us. Head to the Digital Zone and watch the Clean Food Clip 1, which dispenses food handling advice in the 1950s.

THINGS TO DO AND THINK ABOUT

1. Have a go at storyboarding your own public information film. Choose a current topic that the government may want to highlight and use the techniques discussed in this chapter. Be as creative as you can.
2. Some media content is intended to perform a public service.
   a) Describe how media content you have studied is intended to perform a public service. (4 marks)
   b) Explain how at least one key aspect is used to achieve a successful public service advert. You should refer to at least one of: language, narrative, representation, categories, institutions, audience. (6 marks)

ONLINE TEST

Test yourself on this topic at www.brightredbooks.net/subjects

SOCIETY

REFLECTING TIME, PLACE AND EVENTS

When we refer to *society* in media studies we essentially mean reflections of the time and/or place that the text was made, set or *consumed* and any events that may have influenced the content both at the time of production or the time it was set.

ANALYSING MEDIA CONTENT AND LINKING IT TO THE CONTEXT OF SOCIETY

In the question paper part of your exam you will be expected to *analyse media content and link it to the context of society*. This means you will have to do two things:

1. Identify any societal aspects.
2. Decode aspects such as representation and language codes to show your understanding of how either meaning has been created to comment on aspects of society or how society aspects have shaped the construction of the text.

DON'T FORGET

A useful tip is to build up a bank of examples from the start of your course and to widen your understanding of some of the issues you come across. You should keep detailed notes of your examples.

RESEARCH

To discover some aspects of society in the texts you have studied you will have to do some research. You should not rely on just one text to discuss aspects of society, as this would be challenging and you could fail to show depth. You should explore other texts that challenge/parallel or are set against a backdrop of similar society aspects. For example, you could look at gender representation, perhaps from another perspective, or by using an example from another era when ideas surrounding gender were very different. This will allow you to answer your questions with real depth and insight. Remember that you don't have to study the full text to examine good examples of key aspects and that although this chapter focuses on a film example you could equally use non-fiction texts, such as advertising, news content, a film poster, a documentary or a combination of these.

You can also comment on society aspects for the unseen analysis part of your exam. For example, within a film poster the **mise en scène** may be constructed to represent a particular period of history, or a magazine cover may reference celebrities or trends that are current and relevant to today's society. You will not be able to do prior research for this; however, if you have practiced enough examples and know what to look out for, this should be second nature to you.

EXAMPLES OF SOCIETY ASPECTS IN FILM TEXTS

In this section we will consider some examples of society aspects in film texts. There are many societal aspects we could look at, for example:

- different historical events
- political events
- stereotypical ideologies of a particular era, such as depictions of race or social class
- the portrayal of technological advances.

contd

Society – Reflecting time, place and events

Look at the following example.

EXAMPLE:

Huey Military Helicopters flying over a jungle environment during the Vietnam War

Apocalypse Now (1979), inspired by Joseph Conrad's novella 'Heart of Darkness', was both directed and produced by Francis Ford Coppola (*The Godfather* trilogy). Coppola borrowed from other genres such as horror to truly portray the terror of war. Captain Willard (Martin Sheen) embarks on a journey down river on a naval patrol boat accompanied by a surfing fanatic army officer (Robert Duvall) and crazed photographer (Dennis Hopper) to assassinate the power-crazed Colonel Klutz (Marlon Brando) from deep within the Columbian rainforest. The crew of the vessel travel down through the oppressive river into 'the heart of darkness'. The film, as well as being a beautifully shot cinematic experience, is also a comment on the corruption of the Vietnam War, and it is a poignant portrayal of the brutal and corrupt nature of the US involvement in the epic war.

How is it done?

Coppola plays with the use of light in the film and the progressive darkness becomes a metaphor for a lack of civilisation. One of the iconic scenes is the use of military helicopters flying into battle against a soundtrack of Wagner's 'The Ride of the Valkyries', which is being transmitted from radios (use of diegetic sound). Ironically, these helicopters were called back into service during the shoot to deal with rebels on an island nearby, thus blurring fiction with reality. In order to depict the true gore of war the decision was made at one point to use real human remains (from a local research laboratory) as props – although this was later abandoned due to an issue with supply! To reflect the chilling nature of war Coppola created a hallucinatory atmosphere throughout the film (which also reflected the increasingly distressed states of mind of the actors on, what was documented to be, one of the most difficult film shoots in history).

Scenes such as the 'air strike', 'Sampon' and 'bridge strikes' depict death and destruction during Vietnam at the hands of the US troops who appear to fire indiscriminatingly at civilians in order to take control of the land. Central to the film is the hypocrisy that, while civilians and troops are dying on mass, the focus is on the tracking down of one of the highest-ranking military personnel. This is anchored with lines such as, 'We'd cut them in half and give them a Band-Aid' and the brutal killing of a peasant in Sampon.

The film also questions the values of the American soldiers, for example, the scene where the American soldiers' attentions are fixated upon the young local women while the locals calmly eat their simple meal of rice. The scene at the start of the film where soldiers are being filmed in action by a journalist who tells them not to look at the camera has parallels with a time when actual footage of Vietnam was broadcast, suggesting that war can be a form of entertainment. *Apocalypse Now* didn't shy away from events that may be perceived to be morally compromising.

ONLINE

Go to the Digital Zone and read an article on reflection and change as depicted in film – www.brightredbooks.net/subjects

THINGS TO DO AND THINK ABOUT

Watch and research the film *Apocalypse Now*, including the making of the film: 'Heart of Darkness: A Filmmaker's Apocalypse' shot in part by Coppola's wife, and 'Apocalypse'.

In addition, research facts on and societal attitudes towards the Vietnam War. Not only will this thoroughly prepare you for answering a question about society but also give you plenty of material to answer all key aspects, most notably about language, institution and representations. Look also at the case study on page 94 for further information.

ONLINE TEST

Test your knowledge on the BrightRED Digital Zone – www.brightredbooks.net/subjects

SOCIETY

EXAMPLES OF SOCIETY ASPECTS IN FILM TEXTS

> **DON'T FORGET**
>
> Just because a film explores the dark world of war it doesn't mean it is an anti-war film.

WAR IN FILMS

Once you have fully researched *Apocalypse Now* and the Vietnam War, try finding another representation of war either to draw parallels with or show contradictions to *Apocalypse Now*.

You could explore any other war films, such as the examples shown here.

German soldiers at the beginning of the Battle of the Bulge, 1944.

EXAMPLE:

Act of Valor (2012) was directed by Mike McCoy and Steven Waugh and McCoy took the unusual decision to use active duty US navy SEALs and other naval personnel to appear in the film alongside actors. The film focuses on the high-performing squad of elite navy SEALs and, impressive as their performance is, the film does somewhat sanitise the US involvement in the Middle East. It shies away from the gory physical and psychological effects on all of those involved in war. Interestingly, the trailer of *Act of Valor* was shown:

- during a Super Bowl match
- during the popular teen film *Chronicle* (PG-13 in the US)
- at the start of the PlayStation game *Battlefield*.

Think of the target audiences of the above. Many have dubbed the film as the biggest military recruitment propaganda campaign in recent history.

Tip: You could explore this angle for questions on the Role of the Media. This film is also mentioned within the Institutions chapter.

EXAMPLE:

The John Wayne film *The Green Berets* (1968) is an example of an ill-received Vietnam film (made at the time). A cynical reporter (David Janssen) who is opposed to the Vietnam War is sent to cover the conflict and assigned to tag along with a group of Green Berets (United States Army Special Forces). Led by tough-as-nails Colonel Mike Kirby (John Wayne), the team is given a top-secret mission to sneak behind enemy lines and kidnap an important Việt Cộng Commander. Along the way, the reporter learns to respect why America is involved in the war. It was very much in the style of a propaganda movie, but they misjudged the groundswell of opinion against the war and the movie was an epic flop.

Top Gun (1986), directed by Tony Scott, was also suggested to promote military recruitment, as the narrative portrays rather more unrealistic representations of the reality of military life played out by Maverick (Tom Cruise) whose refusal to conform is seen to be tolerated by the US Air Force because he is a talented pilot (being such a catch, he also woos his female flight instructor). This portrays a somewhat distorted version of reality.

Society – Examples of society aspects in film texts

MORE EXAMPLES

Other good examples of films to research for the portrayal of war include:

- *Dunkirk* (2017), director Christopher Nolan
- *Forrest Gump* (1994), director Robert Zemeckis
- *12 Strong* (2018), director Nicolai Fuglsig
- *Black Hawk Down* (2001), director Ridley Scott.

Other suggestions of aspects of society that can be easily explored in film are the rise of fear of terrorism, public mistrust of government and gender roles. Note how closely linked these are with representations and ideologies. Please do some research to come up with ideas of your own.

Aspect of Society Prevalent in the Film	Suggestions of Films
Mental illness 	Many texts deal with this issue but rarely in a positive light. Often, Hollywood depicts a character suffering from mental illness as dangerous or at best completely crazy. Often the horror or psychological thriller genre is used to portray such illnesses. Consider films such as *One Flew Over the Cuckoo's Nest* (1975) (director Milos Forman) or *Shutter Island* (2010) (director Martin Scorsese), where the patients are institutionalised and treated almost like criminals. They both paint a frightening and depressing social comment about the treatment of mental health patients at the time. Compare with modern TV dramas that are better at portraying a more positive depiction of the reality of living with mental illness. Look at programmes such as *Homeland*, *Coronation Street* and *EastEnders* for more normalised portrayals of illnesses such as bipolar disorder and depression. For further reading on this topic and examples of other films read the short publication *Screening Madness* by King's College London, Institute of Psychiatry (www.time-to-change.org.uk/sites/default/files/film-report-screening-madness-time-to-change.pdf), which reveals four classic stereotypes of people with mental health problems.
Poverty 	You could compare the reality of poverty in India in films such as *Slumdog Millionaire* (2008) (director Danny Boyle) and *Trishna* (2011) (director Michael Winterbottom), with poverty in the UK in short social realism film *Wasp* (2003) (director Andrea Arnold) or *I, Daniel Blake* (2016) (director Ken Loach).

THINGS TO DO AND THINK ABOUT

Remember that societal aspects link to themes. During the pre-production stage of your assignment you should think about an aspect of society you might want to explore – *misuse of authority, mental illness, war, playground politics, friendship, the rise of the frenemy* … the possibilities are endless. This should become one of your themes. Only then are you ready to start thinking about how you might be able to portray those themes (on a budget).

Now add to the list above and consider what issues you may want to explore. Beside each one think about how you might show that in content of your choice. Develop one idea by writing a one-page treatment.

DON'T FORGET

Remember you don't only have to identify and comment on the different aspects of society and *how* they are dealt with or reflected in one film alone, but could consider comparing different films. Don't forget to identify the different codes used to portray these events or portrayals.

DON'T FORGET

This is perhaps one of the most interesting aspects of studying media, as all media is always a reflection of, or comment on, some aspect of society. You should thoroughly explore this key aspect of the course!

ONLINE

For further reading on this topic and examples of other films, read the short publication *Screening Madness* by King's College London, Institute of Psychiatry. Head to the Digital Zone for a link to the article – www.brightredbooks.net/subjects

ONLINE TEST

Test yourself on this topic and have a go at answering an exam-style question on the Digital Zone.

AUDIENCE

TARGET AUDIENCE AND AUDIENCE RESEARCH

DON'T FORGET

Audience is a *context-based key aspect*, as are Institutions and Society. Language (camera/lighting/sound/print language), Representations, Narrative and Categories are all *context*-based key aspects.

TARGET AUDIENCE

All media, regardless of the main purpose, is created with a *target audience* in mind, so it is important to find some way of categorising and identifying audiences in order to reach them.

Two ways that media content producers categorise audiences are through **psychographics** and **demographics**.

PSYCHOGRAPHIC CATEGORISATION

Psychographic categorisation works by grouping audiences together according to their values, attitudes and lifestyle choices (VALS). The method of collating the information for this type of study is called *qualitative*. The research is collected using methods such as interviews and focus groups.

These categories do change over time as society's ideas and trends change and it is important to recognise that different cultures have different psychographic categories. The following example of psychographic categories was identified by the company Young & Rubicam for the purpose of advertising:

- *The Aspirer* – I love brands (especially luxury items). Some would go as far as to say I am materialistic or even superficial. Image is very important to me. I am easily persuaded.
- *The Reformer* – I am certainly not materialistic; in fact, I am quite selective with my choices. I think before I buy.
- *The Explorer* – I am quite young or at least young at heart. I enjoy a real challenge and love exciting new brands.
- *The Mainstream* – I am average because I belong to the largest group in society. I love established brands that are tried and tested. Value for money is important to me and I like to feel secure.
- *The Struggler* – As my title suggests, I find it really hard to manage my finances, career and life in general. I am really good at drinking and eating junk food. I also love escapism – anything that helps me forget the mess that is my life. Short-term satisfaction is great for me – it makes me feel better. Until the next mess ...
- *The Succeeder* – Thankfully, I am very different to The Struggler. I am driven, focused and productive and can set goals and achieve. Others see me as responsible and trustworthy. I enjoy prestigious brands because I can afford them – and I deserve them after all of my hard work!
- *The Resigned* – I am usually a little long in the tooth (old). I don't like change and so my brand choices are safe – I stick to what I know. I do love a bit of *nostalgia* though because the old times were the best!

ACTIVITY

For each of the above consider the following questions:

1. What TV programmes do you think that each 'type' would watch?
2. What magazines or newspapers do you think they would read?
3. What type of advertising would you target towards each type – for example, before a film, during programme breaks or in magazines or newspapers?
4. Do you fit into one or more of the 'types'?

Audience – Target audience and audience research

DEMOGRAPHICS

The term 'demographics' refers to another way of categorising the population – this can be done in a number of ways. These categories are measured using data such as age, audience, family status, class, nationality, education, religious beliefs or even the type of work they do. This, again, helps producers discover the needs of the target audience. Demographic data is measured using *quantitative methods* – by numerical values.

Consider the following commonly used socio-economic chart. As you can see it is income based, with the lowest income receivers at the bottom and highest at the top. Remember, the highest earners will have more disposable income and be able to spend more. Categorising in this way will allow advertisers to place their advertisements in the correct places.

Most productions or publications will have a media pack (commonly available on the Internet). If we take *Heat* magazine as an example, we can see that the 'average' reader is female, aged 30 and most likely to be A, B or C1 on the socio-economic scale. Statistically, 47 per cent are single and 48 per cent are married; 56 per cent live in rental accommodation and 46 per cent own their own home; 34 per cent have children under the age of 15.

ACTIVITY

Based on the above information, what type of products do you think might be advertised in *Heat* magazine? Which may not?

ACTIVITY

Research the demographic profile for three publications of your choice from a media pack, for example, *British Vogue, The Sunday Times, The Sun, Hello!, Heat* or *Shout*. Note the *demographic profile* of each and try to *imagine what type of products may be advertised* in each. Consider also what products wouldn't do so well.

ACTIVITY

Consider the following table and fill out as many examples as you can of content or publications that each may engage in. Some have been done for you but see if you can add to them.

A	Higher management, bankers, lawyers, doctors and other such professions	
B	Middle management, teachers, creative and media professionals and so forth	
C1	Office supervisors, junior managers, clerical staff and white-collar workers	
C2	Skilled manual workers	
D	Semi-skilled and unskilled workers	
E	Unemployed, students, pensioners, casual workers	

Category	TV Content or Films Likely to Watch	Magazines or Newspapers Likely to Consume	Type of Adverts that Would be a Good Target
The Struggler		*Gossip* magazine	Gambling helplines, debt consolidation services ...
The Mainstream	*The X Factor*		
The Aspirer	*Made in Chelsea*	*Vogue*	
The Succeeder	*Suits*		
The Explorer			Apple products
The Reformer		*Radio Times*	

DON'T FORGET

These are just guides. We can (and indeed need to) make assumptions about different categories of audience members (based on research) but there will always be exceptions! The type of content one consumes often just comes down to personal taste!

VIDEO LINK

Watch the video on the Digital Zone to explore the topic further – www.brightredbooks.net/subjects

ONLINE TEST

Test yourself on this topic at www.brightredbooks.net/subjects

THINGS TO DO AND THINK ABOUT

1. What do you think are the potential flaws and advantages of each type of categorisation? Consider whether the stereotypes are demeaning or if they miss out any categories of people. Which profile (or profiles) best fit you?

2. You should do your own research (for your assignment) to discover the audience demographics for similar content to your own. And research the target audience for the texts you are studying – this will to a large extent have influenced many of the production decisions that have been made. Click online to download a worksheet to help you organise your audience research.

AUDIENCE

AUDIENCE APPEAL, RESPONSES AND NEEDS 1

AUDIENCE AND TEXT

As mentioned in the previous chapter, it is essential in media studies to consider the relationship between audience and text. All producers need to know their 'target audience' and all texts contain codes and messages to encourage the audience to engage with the content and understand the intended messages in a particular way. Different audiences will interpret the text differently according to their values, experiences and beliefs. In short, media can't exist without an audience.

 ACTIVITY

Before you read on, consider why producers want their texts to appeal to a wider audience.

MODE OF ADDRESS

This simply refers to the method that the producers have used to address or 'speak' to the audience and how they have influenced them.

Texts can be communicated in different ways, as shown below.

Direct	Indirect	Formal	Informal
For example, posters may address the audience using first-person such as 'we', 'you' or 'us' to make them feel involved.	Posters may use a less personal tone, adopting third-person language such as 'they' or 'them'.	In adverts the text could use very formal language.	Informal language may adopt a conversational tone or use slang.
Or a model on a magazine cover may look directly at the camera and therefore the audience. They may have been framed at eye-level to establish a connection. They may use a close-up shot, which feels quite intimate/friendly.	Narration styles may create distance and allow us to experience other worlds. We may experience a narrative from a different character's point of view.	Body language could be formal, perhaps by placing a news reporter behind a desk – such as you may see on a BBC News programme.	Models may adopt a relaxed or informal pose. A news reporter may be standing up or even sitting on the edge of the desk, for example, 5 News.
A documentary-style programme may address the audience directly through a piece to camera, giving the idea of chatting with a friend. Voice-overs may be used to address the audience directly.	On a magazine cover the model may be looking away from the audience or a long shot may be used. The angle of the shots may be high or low angle, positioning us in a place of authority or inferiority to the subject.	Broadsheet newspapers may use formal language and be more *impartial*.	Tabloid newspapers may use a chattier tone and deal with less serious issues. A radio presenter is often informal, chatting directly to the listener as if they know them. Appeal on their behalf 'we' this will establish a connection.

By allowing an audience to see the world from the perspective of a character – for example, directly through the use of point of view (POV) or indirectly by way of reaction shots – the audience can connect with that character, perhaps building sympathy. This is because they experience the world from their perspective. This is called *audience positioning*.

DON'T FORGET

Don't forget to consider why the creators of the text would want you to feel, for example, sympathy. Is it to reinforce the narrative? To identify with a situation? To promote a product? It is important to link audience and purpose.

ACTIVITY

Watch a clip from a film you are studying and try to identify:

- Who does the camera follow?
- What camera angles, distances or movements are used to enforce this perspective?
- What effect does this have on the audience's relationship with the viewer – for example, do we feel involved, distant, sympathetic or unsympathetic?

contd

Audience – Audience appeal, responses and needs 1

EXAMPLE:

This *NME* cover opposite was used in 2011 to commemorate the death of Amy Winehouse. It has become an iconic issue. Amy is looking directly at the camera (direct mode of address) and her stance is relaxed (informal). It captures her edgy personality while also showing a softer side to her. The publication chose not to add anything else to the cover (that is, *splashes* or *pull quotes*), although the logo is still prominent, inherently linking the icon to the brand *NME*. It became one of the most iconic covers in the magazine's history. *NME* ceased publication of the print form of the magazine in 2018.

BREAKING THE FOURTH WALL

Breaking the fourth wall is a term used to describe direct audience address in performance – the fourth wall being the audience. Favoured by Shakespeare, this certainly isn't a new concept, but one that was once considered a cinematic rule never to be broken. Breaking the fourth wall allows a connection with the audience, which means the actor temporarily dropping character to establish a brief and direct connection with the audience, either through dialogue or a direct gaze to the audience. This is a non-realistic device because it is not a natural thing to do in cinema or theatre – the main aim is usually to create a world that is convincing to the audience.

The purpose of establishing this informal and personal link with the audience could be one or more of the following: to function as a storytelling device, to highlight an important issue or theme, to inject humour, to give inside knowledge about a character or situation, as a metaphor or epiphany (sudden realisation) or to present an immediate or live feel to the performance. It is often the marker of an **independent film**, although it is now a popular technique.

 **ACTIVITY**

Head to the Digital Zone and watch the short clip form François Truffaut's *The 400 Blows*, which explores the trauma of growing up from a young boy's perspective. The POV shot at the end appears to deliberately address the audience and encapsulates the boy's state of mind far better than any other narrative or acting could have done. This was referenced in the film *This is England* (2006). Go online for further examples and try to find examples of your own.

ACTIVITY: Research it!

Research the work of filmmaker (and **auteur**!) Woody Allen, including his examples of breaking the fourth wall.

 THINGS TO DO AND THINK ABOUT

Look at the following pictures. Which modes of address have been used to address the reader and to what effect?

a) 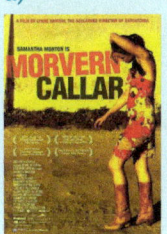   b)    c)

DON'T FORGET

As a filmmaker you should first think about what you are trying to portray to your audience, and *then* consider which of the techniques you have learned best serves that purpose. To pick a device, tempting though it may seem, and run with it just for the sake of it, will result in your final content being gimmicky and probably ineffective in communicating your message in a strong and clear way. Do experiment but consider your approach conservatively; don't throw every technique in this book at your production. Less is often more stylish.

DON'T FORGET

Remember to keep detailed notes of your research for both your assignment and question paper.

VIDEO LINK

Watch a short clip from François Truffaut's *The 400 Blows* on the Digital Zone – www.brightredbooks.net/subjects

ONLINE

Check out examples of breaking the fourth wall at www.brightredbooks.net/subjects

ONLINE TEST

Test yourself on this topic at www.brightredbooks.net/subjects

AUDIENCE

AUDIENCE APPEAL, RESPONSES AND NEEDS 2

PREFERRED READINGS, NEGOTIATED READING AND DIFFERENTIAL DECODING

According to media theorist Stuart Hall, when we are encouraged to read a text in a particular way and accept the messages within the text, we are accepting the '*preferred reading*' – the messages intended by the audience.

However, when we reject (disagree with) the messages and form a different meaning this is referred to as a *differential decoding* (or reading). We unravel messages and codes within the text and create an understanding that is often not what was intended. (This is what good pupils of media studies do!)

If we partly accept the reading and partly reject it, we call it a *negotiated reading*.

EXAMPLE:

To illustrate the idea of different readings, consider the film *Brave*, a 2012 American computer-animated fantasy drama adventure film produced by Pixar Animation Studios and released by Walt Disney Pictures.

Set in medieval Scotland, fiery, red headed, wild-child Merida struggles to conform to the expectations placed upon her to conform to being a princess. The character's charm lies in her spirited attempts to rebel against her mother's wishes for her to behave like a princess and marry a suitable prince.

The *preferred reading* here is of a young princess and her stormy relationship with her mother, the Queen. The producers have used stereotypes to reinforce obvious representations of character type to encourage a preferred reading. The camera follows the young princess as she grows up so the audience are positioned (see page 55) with Merida throughout and gradually build sympathy for her.

Merida has a stereotypical Scottish appearance and demeanour – red hair, pale complexion, speaks with a Scottish accent and is very stubborn. Both her father and mischievous twin brothers have some very unflattering traits, such as their 'cave man' appearance and rather crude manners. They don't appear very domesticated and the youngsters are often seen eating from the floor.

The *disruption stage* of the story reveals a fight with rival clan chiefs over Merida's hand in marriage. Merida is not a stereotypical princess (Disney or otherwise) and audiences liked that, to an extent, she reflects modern times.

DON'T FORGET

All assumptions we make about audience groups are very general – not all American audience-members will read the texts the same way.

ACTIVITY

1. Watch the film and read some reviews on the film before answering the following questions as thoroughly as possible:
   How is Scotland portrayed in the text?
   How are women portrayed through Merida and her mother?
   How are men portrayed in the film?

2. How do you think different audiences may react? Consider the following:

   (a) What is the preferred reading?

   (b) Could there be any differential decoding by audience groups, for example, Scottish audiences, an audience reading from a feminist perspective or American audiences?

Audience – Audience appeal, responses and needs 2

IDENTIFYING A TARGET AUDIENCE

Identifying a target audience can be a tricky job but here are a few questions you can consider to help you. Try this out now with a text you know well.

NOTE: This will be helpful for the question paper part of the exam (including the Unseen Analysis) and your assignment planning section.

- Does it require any specialist knowledge to understand, that is, for technology-aware audiences? Yes → niche audience? No → more global audience?
- Is the language complex or are there any cultural or intertextual references that need prior knowledge? Yes → well-educated audiences?
- Does it highlight or reject any ideologies, representations or traditions, for example, the representation of stereotypical gender roles?
- Is it classified as age specific? For example, iPlayer and other apps now ask viewers to declare that they are over the age of 16 before they can watch the content.
- Is the narrative complex or the themes challenging?
- Have the producers used one or more obvious conventions or a particular genre?
- Does the content lean towards a particular political viewpoint?
- Could the audience be fans of the director or actors?
- Is there a notable cinematography style?

The main thing to take away from this section is that most texts can be read in different ways. You should always consider:

- What types of audience groups may elicit differential readings from a text?
- What those readings are likely to be and how they may have decoded them.

It is important to remember that not every text has a hidden agenda: no two people are the same, so it is completely natural that we all read content in a different way.

 ONLINE

Visit the Digital Zone for more examples of preferred reading and differential decoding – www.brightredbooks.net/subjects

 THINGS TO DO AND THINK ABOUT

Research it!
- Stuart Hall's **encoding**/decoding model and differential reading.
- BBC audience charter to learn about the regulations on subjectivity and being non-biased.
- BBFC age classifications.

 ONLINE TEST

Test yourself on this topic at www.brightredbooks.net/subjects

COURSE ASSESSMENT

THE EXAM QUESTION PAPER

WHAT YOU CAN EXPECT

The National 5 question paper consists of five general questions (50 marks) and an unseen analysis task (10 marks). There is a total of 60 marks available, which is 50 per cent of your total exam result. You have two hours to complete the exam. Although an exam can be nerve-wracking, by the time you reach this stage in your course you should not have anything to worry about. You have studied and examined a variety of texts throughout the year, which will give you more than enough content to cover the exam questions. You know the key aspects (content and context) and can discuss each with reference to an example or several examples of content samples.

Skills, knowledge and understanding

The examination board will assess your knowledge and understanding by giving you an opportunity to *analyse* and discuss content you are familiar with as well as providing you with a choice of three print texts to choose from.

Aim to be concise but detailed enough to show insight in your answers. As well as demonstrating your understanding of how the content has been shaped, you must show why it has been created the way it has – what role is it fulfilling? What are the intended reactions from the audience? What will the preferred reading be, and could there be an unintended reading?

You must be sure to make connections between the content of your example and the context (aspects of society, influence or constraints placed upon the institution and the appeal to, or reactions from, the audience). This is called cause and effect and you will find this term used in the marking instructions. You will also have to demonstrate your understanding of the role of the media.

You should now be very familiar with the key aspects of media literacy and role of the media type questions. As a reminder, at National 5 you could be asked about, and therefore be prepared to answer, any combination of the following:

> categories — genre, purpose, tone
> language — medium-/form-specific technical codes, cultural codes, anchorage
> narrative — medium-/form-specific structures, codes, conventions
> representation — selection and portrayal, stereotypes, non-stereotypes, cultural assumptions.

Media contexts

Context-based key aspects of media literacy:

- audience – target audience, preferred reading, different audience reactions
- institution – internal factors, external factors
- society – time, place (for example, facts, information, ideas, history, circumstances, events, politics, technology or any other factors relevant to the society in which particular examples of media content were made, set or consumed).

Role of media in society

The ways in which media functions within society:

- meeting needs – entertainment, education, information
- achieving particular purposes – profit, promotion, public service
- influencing attitudes and behaviour – intentionally, unintentionally.

(SQA N5 Course Specification; This edition: August 2017, version 2.0)

DON'T FORGET

This may sound overwhelming, but the questions are clearly designed to cover all of these areas – all you have to do is answer them well!

DON'T FORGET

The unseen analysis is covered in depth in the next four chapters and the other questions have been explored throughout the book in the chapters on the key aspects; so, you should now be ready to try the whole paper.

Course assessment – The exam question paper

QUESTION 1

The first five questions in the paper will usually be set out as follows:

> Media content can create stereotypes and/or challenge stereotypes.
>
> a) Describe representations which create and/or challenge stereotypes in media content you have studied. (6 marks)
>
> b) Explain in detail how language features have been used to create and/or challenge stereotypes. (6 marks)

Question a) asks you to identify the representations/stereotypes.

Question b) asks you to show how they are created.

This two-part question helps you to structure your thoughts. You can gain 1 mark for each point you make and 1 mark for developing your answer. (Some questions in your exam will be easy to answer in a series of simple points whereas other questions will lend themselves to a much more developed answer, depending on your strengths, understanding and the content you have studied.)

ACTIVITY

In the example above it should be very easy to identify a variety of six different representations. You could pick obvious gender, racial, age stereotypes/non-stereotypes, or representation of a culture, place or event. This should be very easy – *Do this now*.

The second part of the question makes you work a little harder as you have to carefully and concisely explain in detail *how* each of the representations or stereotypes have been constructed, in this case through the use of language. You may want to discuss technical codes such as camera work and lighting and cultural codes such as costumes or accent. In each case don't forget to work through the connotations of your observations, linking them clearly back to the representation you are explaining (cause and effect) – *Do this now*.

Note: Do be aware that if you have covered SIX points in part a) but your answers to part b) are very detailed and make several extended points each. You will not need to cover all six identified representations. You would either run out of time or find yourself using answers that you may want to use for another question. Pace yourself – you still have the unseen analysis to complete.

QUESTION PAPER – SECTION 2

In section 2, Analysis of a Media Text, you will choose one of three media print texts (see pages 62): a film poster, an advertisement or a magazine front cover. This is worth 10 marks and the question is always the same: 'Explain in detail how relevant aspects of media literacy have been used with particular purpose(s) and for particular audience(s).' (SQA N5 Course Specification; This edition: August 2017, version 2.0)

In your answer you should refer to at least two of the following:

- Language
- Categories
- Audience
- Society
- Representation
- Narrative
- Institution

THINGS TO DO AND THINK ABOUT

Marking instructions used by the SQA marking team can be found on the SQA past paper section of the N5 Media page and a simplified version, with key points, in the 'Further Practice' chapter. Go online to the SQA website (www.sqa.org.uk) and familiarise yourself with these documents so you can be confident of exactly what is expected from you.

DON'T FORGET

You can find all the past papers (with marking instructions) on the SQA website and there are some additional practice questions for you at the back of this book.

DON'T FORGET

Remember that you can use more than one media text to answer your questions.

DON'T FORGET

You will find examples of some previous SQA questions in the Further Practice section. If you get stuck, go back to the chapters that deal with that specific aspect.

DON'T FORGET

There should be absolutely no need to repeat yourself. You will be awarded marks once but not twice just because you have put the same point in different words.

ONLINE

Head to the Digital Zone for a link to the SQA marking instructions www.brightredbooks.net/subjects

COURSE ASSESSMENT
ANALYSING PRINT TEXTS

ANALYSING ADVERTISEMENTS

In your exam you will be asked to deconstruct and analyse an unseen print text – a magazine cover, an advertisement or a film poster. This is an excellent opportunity for you to showcase your knowledge and pick up marks in the exam. You will have to apply your knowledge of how the key aspects combine to create meaning. You will have to explain, analyse and evaluate in your response. The examiners will require you to go beyond merely identifying the key aspects (although this will most certainly be a good starting point). A strong answer will show depth (detail) and breadth of understanding (a variety of key aspects) as well as overall insight (original and perceptive ideas). You must justify your opinions with clear and detailed reference to the text.

It is important not to go any further until you are very confident with your knowledge of the key aspects. Before you continue, take a moment to revise the key aspects and subsets, i.e. categories such as genre, purpose, tone, form, medium and style.

KEY ASPECTS AND ANALYSING ADVERTISING

Remember that the key aspects are all interdependent. This means, rather than existing in isolation, they *link* and *combine* to create meaning.

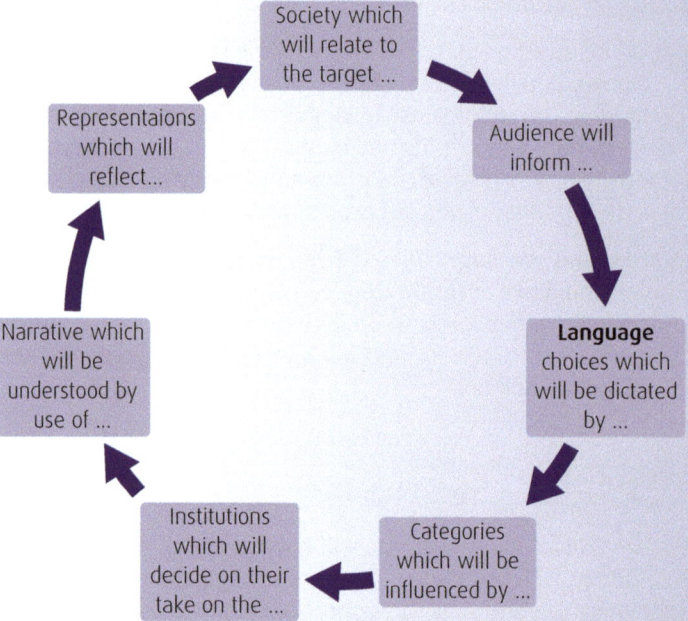

This is only one combination; the arrows can connect in any direction! The key to analysing any text is to remember that every choice is intentional. Advertisements will be selling you a lifestyle by trying to tap into your greatest desires, fears and insecurities. One of the techniques that enables advertisers to do this is by using one or more of the following *lines of appeal*:

- Happy Families
- Luxurious and affluent lifestyles
- Dreams and fantasy
- Romance and Love
- Glamorous places
- Influential people or 'experts'
- Successful careers
- Art, culture and history
- Nature and the natural world
- Beautiful people
- Self-importance and pride
- Comedy and humour
- Ideals of childhood

(Dyer, G., *Advertising as Communication*, 1988, Routledge)

This helps the advertisers anchor certain values to the brand.

contd

Course assessment – Analysing print texts

 **ACTIVITY**

Identify any lines of appeal (there may be more than one) used in the adverts below and try to work out what, if any, values are attached to the brand.

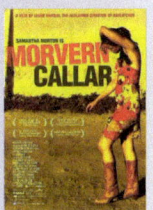  

Remembering that you have to go beyond identifying the key aspects, ask yourself the following simple questions to help give your answer structure and enough depth.

Question	Things to Consider
1. *What* is the purpose of the advert?	For example: profit, promotion, public service …
2. *Who* is the target audience?	*Demographics*: average audience members status (usually linked to job) and *psychographics*: age, gender, race and other categories.
3. *What* is being advertised and how?	Any relevant, form-specific language codes, for example: layout of text; main image and *pack shots*; position of images and whether they are literal or metaphorical; colours; *eye-line vectors*; framing, distance and angle of photography in relation to audience (for example, is the subject given authority over the audience by the use of a low-angle shot?); cultural codes; representations; any obvious genre clues (if relevant); narrative; tone: *intertextuality* or *parody* (does it make reference to any other media text?); any call to action; slogan; brand identity; or any other additional information. Remember you can use the AIDA acronym to help you with the analysis of your text.
4. *How* this helps to sell the product.	How the text meets the needs of the audience (for example, you could consider Maslow's Hierarchy of Needs); influences behaviour and attitudes; reflects society aspects by presenting any lines of appeal (see above) to reflect modern life or old-fashioned values/traditions.

 **ONLINE**

For further information on pack shots and eye-line vectors, head to the Digital Zone.

DON'T FORGET

Don't forget to collect a file of adverts that you enjoy or that you think are effective. The more you study, the better you will get at analysing and understanding any hidden messages.

WORKING OUT A SOLUTION

Example of Answer	Comment
The film poster for *Morvern Callar* uses three main colours: red, amber and brown. The colours are muted and earthy, which helps the character blend into her surroundings. The colours help the audience to place the setting of the scene to a hot country, as the warm amber colours have connotations of summer and the red of heat.	This is a perfectly acceptable answer but is unlikely to gain any more than 1 mark. The point here is that the colours help inform the audience of the location of one of the scenes. Basic (underdeveloped point) = 1 mark
In addition, the character is presented as somewhat *enigmatic* – the target audience immediately wonder what her story is. This is achieved through representations and narrative. We assume by her close proximity to the title of the film, that the girl in the poster is Morvern. She is portrayed as stereotypically attractive to a Western audience: slim, bronzed with long dark hair and painted red nails, her dress is figure hugging and colourful, setting her apart from the harsh, arid, bleak landscape surrounding her. This is an example of a binary opposition and creates an *incongruous mismatch* – she seems out of context, as if she doesn't belong, thus adding to the mystery. It is hoped that the questions the image poses, in combination with the other information on the poster, will spark enough curiosity in the audience to view the film.	This develops the first basic point, helping to demonstrate a deeper understanding of the whole text, and would be *worth a further 2 marks*. The main points we discuss here identify the use of narrative codes (Barthes' enigma codes) and we add substance to our answer by briefly mentioning the representation of an attractive female character.
We learn more about the main character through the camera work. Morvern is walking into the shot, which gives an interesting sense of movement, but her pose – which is somewhat alluring – shows she is in no hurry. She appears thoughtful and again we wonder why. This would further attract and hold the interest of the target audience. 1 mark	A further relevant point, discussing the technical codes of camera, developed in more detail. 1 mark

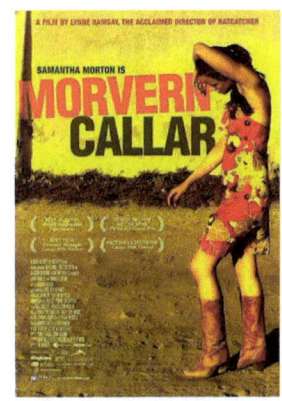

 THINGS TO DO AND THINK ABOUT

Try to find another 6 marks. You could consider developing the representation of Morvern through camera work and position in relation to the audience (consider distance of shot and why she has been presented side on) rather than the often-used pose of addressing the audience face on. Also consider font, acclaimed credits, likely genre, target audience and anything else you notice.

COURSE ASSESSMENT

HOW TO TACKLE UNSEEN ANALYSIS 1

ADVERTISEMENTS

Having been given a selection of three texts to choose from (*film poster, an advertisement and a magazine front cover*) you will be asked a question similar to the one below:

> 'Media texts are made with a particular *purpose* and for specific *audiences*. With reference to purpose and/or audience explain in detail how relevant key aspects of media literacy have been used in your chosen text.
>
> In your answer you must refer to at least two of the following key aspects in relation to purpose and audience:
>
> Language; Representation; Categories; Narrative; Audience; Institution; Society.'

The number of available marks = 10

Important

Remember – 1 mark for each (detailed) point explained then further point/s for each development. You must link ideas showing how one idea affects another (cause and effect).

The key to gaining full marks in this section is the ability to develop the points you make in order to ensure that you are doing enough for the number of marks available. If you are not careful, you could write a lot and find that you have only covered one point, which is only awarded 1 mark, or that you have simply repeated the same idea in a different way gaining no extra credit.

Be concise and develop your answer with new information, a further connected example (to reinforce your line of thought) or a new point. *Never limit yourself to discussing only one key aspect throughout your analysis or you will only gain a maximum of 5 marks.* This is covered in more detail in 'The Exam' section, where you will also find the marking instructions used by SQA to assess your work. The following may help to guide you through an analysis.

AIDA

AIDA

A good advert should: attract the reader's attention so that they stop and read it, hold their interest so that they take a closer look and finally convince them to take action (en.wikipedia.org; accessed 8 January 2018). The *AIDA* model, thought to be first introduced by *St Elmo Lewis* in 1898 and still used in marketing and advertising today, is a simple framework to help you analyse a print text. If you use this approach as a guide, it may help you to organise your thoughts quickly and allow you to apply your knowledge of other key aspects to work out the *purpose, preferred reading* or any *differential decoding*.

A – How does the advertisement first grab our *attention*? Language codes such as image, font and colour?

I – In what ways does it hold our *interest* and encourage us to look further? Background information, foreground, narrative codes (think about the story/message).

D – How does the advertisement try to create *desire*? Promoting value, that is, this season's beauty must haves and bargain buys, celebrity gossip, stereotypes, **denotations**, ideologies ...

A – Can you identify a call for *action*? Websites, phone numbers, release date for film ...

DON'T FORGET

You will still have to discuss the use of the key aspects – AIDA is merely a framework to help you do that.

contd

Course assessment – How to tackle unseen analysis 1

Arrangement – the way the elements of the text have been organised. Is there text right next to the product? This could be very suggestive or anchor meaning; look for repetition of ideas or elements such as colour; any obvious contrasts (for example, between character and setting or two characters) that could be key in creating a narrative.

 **ACTIVITY**

Choose an advert and work through it using AIDA.

Examples of allocation of marks

It is very important that you are clear about what constitutes a developed point.

The following three chapters will provide examples, with suggestions, to help you develop your analysis skills for the three types of texts you will have to choose from in the exam.

The car is *framed* upside down at the top of the page. Its headlamps look like eyes and are *looking directly at the audience* through the dark. It appears as if it has flown to the top of the page/(the ceiling) by itself. It has taken on the appearance of a strange creature, *anchored* by the 'Happy Halloween' *text*. The creators have relied heavily on *enigma narrative codes* to keep the *audience* trying to work out what the car is meant to be. As well as holding the interest of the audience, it establishes a *fun, playful tone*. It is unusual for a car advert and suggest *target audience* like to be unique too.

The idea of the car being alive is again anchored by the *tag line* at the bottom of the poster: 'We only come out at night' and 'Happy Halloween'.

The creators are using Halloween to show the fun side of the Mini. By *representing* the car as a mischievous and fun character it suggests real personality. It is not a boring car and not for boring people. The car looks quite sporty and this suggests performance. This car can go anywhere – *connoting freedom and fun*. Again, unique selling points directed at the target audience.

The layout of the advert is unusual. We notice a large black empty space where we expect to see the main subject of an advert (the car). It draws our attention to the car at the top.

The monochrome colour palette is very stylish and reflects the colours of the car. The message is that the owner of this car will be stylish also.

This advert presents at first as if it isn't even an advert – just a bit of fun. The reality is of course it is an extremely clever and persuasive advert. It uses *lines of appeal* to sell a lifestyle. The person who buys this car will be stylish, fun, young at heart, with a sense of adventure.

The text is a simple *Sans Serif style* and has an almost childlike quality. It is bold and eye-catching.

Playful suggestion again to 'come out to play' in a mini. Potentially aiming at a young audience. The word choice of 'night' has connotations of adventure, reinforcing the idea that the car is fun and suggesting that its owner also lives life on the edge.

The *logo* stands out clearly. No fuss or explanation. This is a confident *brand* and the word 'Mini' is enough. It assumes everybody is already familiar with the brand and shows their confidence in the product. The shape is similar to a bat, which is *anchored* by the tagline 'Happy Halloween'. Reinforcing the light-hearted tone.

 THINGS TO DO AND THINK ABOUT

Work through the examples in the next three chapters and try to add in ideas of your own. Then do the same for examples of your own.

 VIDEO LINK

Visit www.brightredbooks.net/subjects and watch a short video reminder on AIDA.

COURSE ASSESSMENT

HOW TO TACKLE UNSEEN ANALYSIS CONT'D

MAGAZINE COVER

Another option you will be offered in the Unseen Analysis part of your exam is a magazine front cover. Remember, you will have to choose from *at least* two key aspects (see the reminder on pTK). This does not mean you have to stick to only two. Choose from the content-based key aspects – language, representation, categories, narrative – and the context-based key aspects – audience, institutions and/or society. You have to show your knowledge and understanding of the above and show how they work both together and in the context of the poster to create meaning and purpose.

As in the other sections this part of the question paper is worth *10 marks*.

Useful tips

You do not need to be familiar with the magazine cover or content to make it a good choice for you to analyse. The example will have been carefully selected so that there is plenty you can say.

DON'T FORGET

If you only cover one key aspect, you can only be awarded a maximum of 5 marks! Before you look at the text you should first remind yourself of the marking instructions which can be found on the SQA's website.

ONLINE

Head to the Digital Zone for a link to the full SQA marking scheme – www.brightredbooks.net/subjects

First: layout. Remember AIDA: attention, interest, desire and action! How does a magazine cover do that? Here are some examples.

Flash – showing an incentive to buy – 'free CD'

Main image (band) and their name 'Kings of Leon'.

Mug shot with cover lines – in this case widens audience appeal with punk band 'SEX PISTOLS' and 'TRENT REZNOR'.

Prominent placement of masthead (also has to be seen when stacked on shelves).

Pull quote – quote from within the magazine, which the publishers hope will capture the target audience enough to get them to buy and read the full article.

Price and date of issue.

Make sure you address the key aspects in detail.

 **ACTIVITY**

Using the table on page 65 to help you, write a couple of lines on each of the key aspects for the magazine above.

contd

64

Course assessment – VOGUE

Categories – genre, purpose, style, medium, form, tone	Genre – music magazine. What would you expect to find on the front cover of a music magazine?
	Purpose – for profit. How? By creating content to interest their audience and good value for money.
	Tone – this isn't always easy to see but you are being invited to get to know 'Kings of Leon on tour' and their poses are quite relaxed. Can you guess?
Language – technical and cultural codes and anchorage	Look at the framing, especially distance between us and the subject. It is a medium shot but feels quite personal. This has allowed us a privileged insight into the world of the band. Consider the colours or lack of them.
Narrative	Look at all the elements of the layout of the page. Are colours in images reflected in text? Look at the proximity of text to images. Look for enigmas and binary oppositions. Look for the story.
Representations	Look for obvious stereotypes or non-stereotypes, for example, of the music industry or the 'rock 'n' roll world', or any other person or idea represented.
Institutions	You may not know much about the institution in an exam. You should research MOJO for this task. Look also for obvious constraints of genre or form.
Audience	Look at the direct address to the audience. Are the poses formal or informal? What does that say about the tone?
	How else have they tried to engage or appeal to the readers? Look for preferred reading or different audience reactions.
Society	Look for attitudes of society (attitudes of time, place, events).

ONLINE

Visit the Digital Zone for a link to try the unseen analysis specimen paper published by SQA – www.brightredbooks.net/subjects

THINGS TO DO AND THINK ABOUT

The striking April 2008 edition of Vogue, featuring basketball star LeBron James and Brazilian model Gisele Bundchen, sparked some controversy. Before you read through the comments have a look at the cover here https://archive.vogue.com/issue/20080401. Can you work out why it caused so much debate?

(**LANGUAGE**) The long shot of the couple is framed at a slightly high angle – this makes LeBron seem really powerful. His commanding stance and expression reflects the theme of health – he is strong and at his peak.

(**REPRESENTATION**) His stance has been likened to the *King Kong* film poster – and there was some controversy. He was the first black man to be on the front cover of Vogue. His expression is wild and he seems primitive, almost brutish. It is an obvious reading though and some could be offended. A preferred reading is that he is unstoppable, strong, in peak physical condition – he is inspirational. Gisele looks almost weak in his grasp – again some found this distasteful. She is a model, clearly very slim, and looks both healthy and happy. People who buy this are interested in keeping fit and looking good.

The *logo* stands out clearly. This is a recognised *publication* and title needs no embellishment. The red of the title is repeated twice on the cover. In the text, this gives a uniform and polished feel. *Vogue* represents style and the cover reflects that.

This advert clearly tries to appeal to its target audience. We know (from the press pack) that the target audience (readers) that read this are fairly affluent with decent amount of disposable income. It uses *lines of appeal* to sell a lifestyle. The person who buys this magazine will aspire to be stylish, fit and attractive. They will probably be cash rich and time poor. 'The Power of an Hour' and 'No-exercise diet' suggestions would appeal to their target audience perfectly.

They address the audience directly both through the direct look to camera and use of second person – 'You'. Audience expect this; they want to feel as if the magazine is relatable.

There are (NARRATIVE) codes at work here. Binary oppositions have been used. He is black: she is white. He is huge: she is tiny. He looks wild: she looks very placid. He is dressed in black connoting strength and masculinity; she is dressed in light green satin type fabric connoting luxury and femininity. There is a sense of enigma – why is he holding her like a rag doll or his prey? The two contrast but are very both fit and attractive. There is a mock sense of edginess and danger anchored by the red (connoting anger or perhaps passion) masthead 'Vogue'. They go together well anchored by 'perfect fit'. The overall tone is fun and playful.

The layout of the advert is not unusual for a front cover. It is designed to spark your interest and offer value for money.

It is clearly aimed to the fashion conscious. This is the SHAPE ISSUE. Everything on the front cover relates to health and looks. '87 swimsuits to flatter every figure' – not excluding any reader there! 'Dressing for every shape sizes 0–16' is again a move away from the usual typical *Vogue* model figure, which few women can relate to.

COURSE ASSESSMENT

HOW TO TACKLE UNSEEN ANALYSIS CONT'D

FILM POSTER

The film poster is a great choice for your unseen analysis. There will be plenty of opportunities to discuss categories as well as most of the other key aspects. If you have studied film this year you will find much of this text familiar to you. The job of the poster is to attract audience and promote film and you must keep this in mind. Often, it is the first impression the target audience get of the film. It matters. In order for the poster to be a success it must be eye catching, appeal to a wide audience and capture the essence of the film. The set photographer will be present during filming and spend a lot of time capturing photographs for promotional purposes.

Remember that you will have to work through at least two of the key aspects. You should start with a *comment* (for example, the colours that have been used – describe them clearly and note, for example, any repetition, lack of colour or any one colour that stands out) (1 mark). Don't move on to any code or key aspect until you have fully explored/developed this point as much as you can. Recognise and make clear any connotations of meaning (perhaps the colours clearly suggest a particular tone and the effect of those connotations on, for example, audience understanding or clarity of purpose) (another 1 mark).

Describe, *explore connotations* and *link* to function, that is, to clearly define genre in a way that the audience will recognise: to create intrigue so that the audience will want to find out more or to make clear the release date or draw attention to the actors/director.

ACTIVITY

Some suggestions have been made for the *Morvern Callar* poster. Work through them and see what you can add. Try to find another 6 marks. You could consider developing the representation of Morvern through camera work and position in relation to the audience (consider distance of shot and why she has been presented side on) rather than addressing the audience face on. Also consider font, acclaimed credits, likely genre, target audience and anything else you notice. When you have completed this exercise, you should try the example on the next page.

> **DON'T FORGET**
>
> As ever, the key to success is to practice (as much as possible before the exam).

Note: A useful *self-assessment* exercise when you have completed your analysis is to go back through and highlight each key aspect you have used. This will ensure you have discussed more than two and it will highlight any gaps – which may give you further ideas for development of your answer.

contd

Course assessment – How to tackle unseen analysis cont'd

The film poster for *Morvern Callar* uses three main colours: red, amber and brown. The colours are muted and earthy, which helps the character blend into her surroundings. The colours help the audience to place the setting of the scene to a hot country, as the warm amber colours have connotations of summer and the red of heat.	This is a perfectly acceptable answer but is unlikely to gain any more than 1 mark. The point here is that the colours help inform the audience of the location of one of the scenes. *Basic (underdeveloped point) = 1 mark*
In addition, the character is presented as somewhat *enigmatic* – the target audience immediately wonder what her story is. This is achieved through representations and narrative. We assume by her close proximity to the title of the film that the girl in the poster is Morvern. She is portrayed as stereotypically attractive to a Western audience: slim, bronzed with long dark hair and painted red nails, her dress is figure hugging and colourful, setting her apart from the harsh, arid, bleak landscape surrounding her. This is an example of a binary opposition and creates an *incongruous mismatch* – she seems out of context, as if she doesn't belong, thus adding to the mystery. It is hoped that the questions the image poses, in combination with the other information on the poster, will spark enough curiosity in the audience to view the film.	This develops the first basic point helping to demonstrate a deeper understanding of the whole text, and would be *worth a further 2 marks*. The main points we discuss here identify the use of narrative codes (Barthes' enigma) and we add substance to our answer by briefly mentioning the representation of an attractive female character.
We learn more about the main character through the camera work. Morvern is walking into the shot, which gives an interesting sense of movement, but her pose – which is somewhat alluring – shows she is in no hurry. She appears thoughtful and again we wonder why. This would further attract and hold the interest of the target audience. (1 mark) **Development…**	A further relevant point, discussing the technical codes of camera, developed in more detail. (1 mark)

ONLINE

Learn more by researching the film and Scottish film director Lynne Ramsay on the Digital Zone – www.brightredbooks.net/subjects

DON'T FORGET

As media students you should try to use the vocabulary that accurately describes the content or application of the key aspects. Don't be afraid of the jargon!

 ## THINGS TO DO AND THINK ABOUT

It may seem obvious but the more examples you look at the better you will be at the tasks when it comes to the exam. Always keep an eye out for interesting adverts and have a go at working through a key aspects analysis.

 ### ONLINE TEST

Test yourself on this topic at www.brightredbooks.net/subjects

COURSE ASSESSMENT

THE ASSIGNMENT

The assignment is one of the best parts of the media course and most certainly something that you should enjoy. You will be spending a great deal of time on this part of your course, so it is very important that you choose your project carefully – don't just commit to the first idea you have. Your assignment is worth an overall 50 per cent of your overall award (60 marks).

This element of the course is designed to assess how well you can apply the key aspects of media that you have learned throughout your course (as well as serving to consolidate your knowledge before the final exam). It will also test your ability to problem-solve (both during the planning and production stages) and your ability to evaluate both your performance and content.

STAGES OF THE ASSIGNMENT PROCESS

There are four stages of the assignment process.

1. You will be given a *brief* by your teacher that you will have to make a number of decisions about developing. Once you have an idea about how you are going to develop your content, you will have to research all stages of the planning pre-production process.

2. You will have to develop your content. The final finish will be decided between you and your teacher, but you are not required to fully develop moving image to full post-production stage at National 5. Although you may enjoy making the final film it is important to consider your time commitments as it is better to submit a very detailed planning portfolio rather than one that has been rushed in order to fit in the filming of an epic production with a cast of thousands – keep it real!

3. You then have to create the content according to the decisions you have made in your planning and research stages.

4. Finally, you have to evaluate the finished content. What worked and why? What didn't work and how you could have done it better?

You must always do these steps in order and finish one step before you progress to the next – it will be very obvious to your marker if you try to skip the planning stage and do it retrospectively!

Section 1 – Planning section is worth 25 marks and Section 2 – Development is worth 35 marks.

You can choose print or moving image but it is worth thinking about the content you have become most familiar with throughout the duration of your course. If you have become familiar with language codes specific to print advertising, for example, it makes sense to transfer those skills to your assignment rather than try to develop content with which you are unfamiliar.

You can work collaboratively as a group or individually – your teacher will give you guidance on this. If you are working individually you can ask for other pupils to assist as long as you are making all of the decisions and taking full responsibility.

The full instructions for the assignment will be given to you by your teacher but they are also available on the SQA Media N5 website if you want to prepare in advance.

contd

Course assessment – The assignment

In short, you will first decide on the direction your production will take (negotiate the brief) considering stimulus or instruction, target audience and the level of finish (agreed with your teacher). You should keep all notes/sketches/photos or practice films you have shot in order to progress to the next stage. A good candidate will be thinking about possible assignment ideas from the very start of the course – if not before!

You are then ready to research, and you should not underestimate the time this takes!

The research areas are as follows:

- Audience Research – use the audience section to help you identify your audience; assess their needs and work out the best approach to appeal to them. It would be helpful to look at similar content and work out the audience demographics, as you could safely assume it would work for you, too. Audience focus groups and surveys are another approach.

- Institutional research – internal institutional factors such as available equipment/school regulations regarding filming/health and safety/equipment available to you. Use your imagination; there are many great films made without professional cameras and the lack of lighting equipment could work in your favour (see lighting section (pTK)).

- External institutional factors – such as ASA/BBFC/copyright/health and safety and any other legal and voluntary controls.

- Content research – again, if you are keeping careful notes of the content you are studying and perhaps any further examples recommended by your teacher or from the same director/similar genre and so forth, this part of the planning stage should be easy. You want to look for content that has similar themes of style to your own or that inspires you in some way. No content is ever original, and many productions pay *homage* to other works (this is not the same as copying). Think about how the creators have used various key aspects to create effect and meaning. You are asked to choose two aspects from: categories, language, narrative and representation.

You now have to finalise your plans in light of your research. This means that for each bit of relevant research you carried out you want to make a planning decision about your content.

It may be that one piece of research gave you several planning decisions, and that is completely fine. You do need five planning decisions for each of the five sections mentioned above for a total of 25 marks.

You are now ready to make your content!

Finally, you will have to select five (of your best) examples from your content. This is your chance to tell the marker what you were trying to convey through your choice so don't sell yourself short. They only have your plans and content in front of them; if it didn't quite work out, don't worry. You must explain in detail your intentions behind each of your selected decisions as well as evaluate their strengths and/or weaknesses.

The development section is worth 35 marks in total.

DON'T FORGET

Don't be afraid to look at other content – for example, if you are making print adverts to highlight an issue such as mental health you could look at the use of colour in the short film *Le Ballon Rouge* (The Red Balloon) (1956) by Albert Lamorisse, the style of which could easily be transferred to print – colour on black and white can 'pop' and perhaps be symbolic of hope or positivity (for example). Be creative.

ONLINE

Go online to the Digital Zone for examples of assignment work/media production templates/storyboard templates/production roles/production schedule templates and pre-production/post-production assessment sheets and other useful production tools!

THINGS TO DO AND THINK ABOUT

You can access previous SQA candidates' assignment work through the SQA media understanding standards website.

Good luck!

COURSE ASSESSMENT
ASSIGNMENT 1 – PRE-PRODUCTION

PRE-PRODUCTION

Planning and developing media content

Your choice of content will be determined (in part) by the brief given to you by your teacher, although you still have plenty of decisions to make.

Here is an example of a brief (which may also be called a stimulus or instruction):

> Create a short film about a topic that is relevant to teenagers from the age of 13 to 18; of any gender, race or nationality; that will be suitable for screening in a school environment. Your film should be no more than three minutes long. You must make the content individually, although you can direct a small crew should you need help. The film should be suitable to be shown at assembly for S1–6.
> - Budget – £0.
> - Equipment – any additional footage will be shot using the school iPads (or your own camera phones if you wish) and you may edit on Windows Movie Maker, iMovie or any other editing software you may have access to.
> - Health and safety – health and safety guidelines should be adhered to at all times.
> - Time – the deadline for completion is ….

This is a nice open brief because it gives you lots of freedom. You would have to decide on the medium, form, genre, style and topic etc. The age certificate is non-negotiable and will limit your choices to a certain degree. This will also determine, in part, your target audience. You must stick to the instruction to highlight a topic that is important to Scottish teenagers and you mustn't exceed the expected length. Your finished piece of media will be submitted to SQA.

Note: Your teacher may supply you with a brief that is more (or less) prescriptive. The medium may not have been specified, allowing you to create print content as well as moving image.

ACTIVITY: Negotiating the brief

In pairs, come up with a few ideas for possible content.

Consider the following aspects.

Target audience
Who is your trailer aimed at? Think about things like the content, the lead characters, the setting and the genre to help you decide who you should target. Consider audience segments, needs and expectations.

Purpose
The film should raise and highlight an important issue (*inform*). You must also engage your target audience enough to want to watch the full film, so it has to be *entertaining*.

You will need to decide early on in the pre-production stage how you propose to do this, that is, to inform you may want to: use the voice of 'experts' perhaps affirmed by their academic qualifications on the subject; statistics that you may have to manipulate to suit; observational or 'fly-on-the-wall'-style film-making techniques such as video diaries or embed cameras. Your choice of story should be engaging and tackle important aspects of society heads on. To entertain, you may consider a more conventional film-making style and rely on language techniques such as technical and cultural codes, traditional narrative techniques (such as the use of enigmas), representations and stereotypes.

Genre: Think about genre conventions you are familiar with and whether that genre (or elements of the genre) will work for you. Remember you can combine different genres to suit. Don't be afraid to experiment.

ONLINE
Visit the Digital Zone for guidelines on how to write a synopsis – www.brightredbooks.net/subjects

contd

Course assessment – Assignment 1 – pre-production

Plot: You must have a very clear outline of your plot before you embark on your research and final planning decisions. Because you still have to meet the needs of your audience you will have to keep an open mind about the finer details. It may be that you have an alternate ending that you want the audience to choose, for example.

It is useful at this point to get all of your ideas down on one sheet of paper so that you know exactly what it is you are planning for. The best way to do this is to write a synopsis (a short description of your screenplay, highlighting main characters, plot points and setting).

FINALISING YOUR PLAN

You are now ready to finalise your planning. For the N5 Assignment, you must respond to five questions about each area of your research and explain how your findings influenced your plan. The areas, which can be found on the N5 Media website under 'coursework', are: audience, internal institutional factors, external institutional factors, key aspect one and key aspect two.

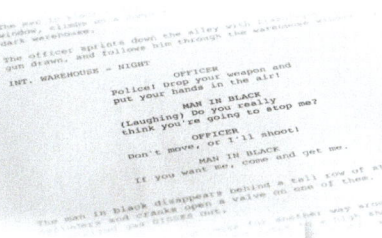

Research

The research sections for N5 are as follows.

Note: The exemplars in this chapter refer to film but the same applies for print content.

1. Audience research – you could carry out an audience survey
Suggested tasks could include identifying similar media content across various platforms and identifying characteristics of your target audience; research the target audience and demographics of the typical audience for the type of content you are thinking of producing. Consider age ratings and so scheduling positions of content similar to yours to gauge audience age. Use the Audience Uses and Gratification Model to identify why your audience will engage with your text. Research social media/comments sections to find information on audience responses. Examine Maslow's Hierarchy of Needs to identify your audience's needs. Conduct a focus group comprised of people who would be within your demographic range. Survey people within your demographic range. Create an audience profile.

2. Internal institutions
Consider time, budget, equipment, expertise or lack of and school regulations and research how others making similar content as you have dealt with budgetary constraints. Avoid merely ranting about the lack of budget in this section as this will lead to a very basic and potentially weak answer. A lack of resources could (and should) allow you to be more creative.

3. External institutions
Research ASA/BBFC and copyright guidelines etc.

Key aspects 1 and 2

Five examples of content you have seen that have inspired and influenced your use of language and technical codes. If you have followed this guide you will have researched plenty of content by this stage; do use the previous research and develop ideas of you own.

For each section you should aim for five different points as this will help structure your response. These could be planning decisions and justifications or a development on one idea. You can also pick up a mark for an additional piece of research. If you have no research or no planning decisions the maximum you can be awarded is two marks. If you need a reminder, go back to each section.

ONLINE

There are several examples that pupils have previously used on the Bright Red Digital Zone.

ONLINE

Head to www.brightredbooks.net/subjects to find a template that shows you the format to use when setting out a script.

ONLINE

Visit the Digital Zone to read on medium and format and scriptwriting essentials – www.brightredbooks.net/subjects

DON'T FORGET

Your storyboard and script should work hand in hand. The final draft of the script would normally be completed before the storyboard.

ONLINE TEST

Test yourself on this topic at www.brightredbooks.net/subjects

THINGS TO DO AND THINK ABOUT

The best way to become good at scriptwriting is to see how others have done it (well). The BBC's writers' room is an excellent resource for those interested in scriptwriting (remember a script doesn't have to include dialogue). Follow the link online for some excellent tutorials on getting you started and access to a number of BBC scripts.

COURSE ASSESSMENT
ASSIGNMENT 2 – PRODUCTION

PRODUCTION

You have now reached the development part of the assignment where you will make your content. The following outlines some suggestions to help you with this stage. As always, planning and organisation are key. At National 5 you don't have to complete a fully finished product – this means if you were planning a film, you could submit the plans and a detailed storyboard. Although this may save you time in the short term, it is harder to evaluate something that you haven't actually made and you may find the final step of your assignment trickier.

PLANNING

The advantage of working thoroughly and systematically through your planning stage is that you will find this part of the assignment much easier.

If you are working on print content, you are pretty much ready to sit down at your PC and put all of your ideas together. Make sure you have all of your notes and research beside you (you must work from your plans because your content and planning should match). It is likely that you will deviate from your plans slightly as you proceed, but you shouldn't produce entirely different content to that suggested in your planning stage. Don't worry if your content doesn't turn out the way you had envisaged; you will have an opportunity to explain your thoughts in the next stage. You can still gain full marks even if things don't go according to plan.

DON'T FORGET

It is crucial that you remember that you are producing print content. The product is almost irrelevant. There is nothing in the assignment instructions that asks you to create a product or to undertake research on that product so you cannot be awarded marks for this approach. So, if your brief is to advertise a car, it is the poster that is assessed – not the car!

STORYBOARDS

If you are producing a film, you will have a bit more to think about. By now you should have a synopsis of your film, research notes and preferably a script. You now need a detailed storyboard. Give each scene on your script a frame until you have worked your way through the entire script. This is where you will want to use your knowledge of film codes to help you.

EXAMPLE: overview

EXT/carpark	Exterior (EXT)/Interior (INT)
Scene description Superman arrives	Keep it brief
Camera ... Long shot, eye level, tripod	Angle/Distance/Movement
Lighting ... Natural day light	Any lighting details
Sound ... None (voice-over post-production)	Any sound details
Timing – 00.01–00.05	Useful for editing

DON'T FORGET

Use sticky notes until you have decided on the best order and the best selection of shots to use, and then draw them onto the storyboard.

ONLINE

Go to www.brightredbooks.net/subjects to see an example of a storyboard.

A properly developed storyboard with space for any production notes will help you stick to the plan and help you write the next stage of the assignment.

contd

Next it would be a good idea to plan a shooting schedule. This means you plan all of your shots in the most sensible order. Note this won't be in the order of your film. You must have a practical approach to filmmaking. It would be more sensible to shoot all of the shots from each location before moving on, or maybe shoot all of the shots required for cast members to avoid them having to return the next day. There are many shooting schedules online but a simple one with the following headings would work just as well.

Shooting Schedule. Name:					
Production Title:					
DATE	SCENE No.	INT/EXT	LOCATION	CAST	NOTES

Plan for every eventuality and always have a back-up plan. Check that your equipment works, is charged (carry a spare charger if you can) and make sure you (or your camera person) know how to use it. Check travel times and make sure that you have done a **recce** of the location beforehand so that there are no nasty surprises. Your cast and crew (if you have any) will be helping you out so look after them. If you can't afford snacks or refreshments for them make sure they know they have to bring a packed lunch/money. Filming days can be long (and boring) for the cast and you don't want them to get fed up halfway through!

Shooting tips: You are no longer an amateur; you are a media student. Follow the tips below but don't forget that your inspiration should be from content you have studied.

More advice

Don't	Do
Point the camera and pan from shot to shot.	Stop and set up each individual shot according to your storyboard.
Use the zoom button on the camera unless you really meant to.	Stop. Cut to a close-up (or medium close-up etc).
Hold the camera unless you have a very good reason for wanting a hand-held effect.	Use a tripod. Or a cushion on a table. You can make a tabletop cardboard tripod quite easily. There are many links online or use the one from into film (www.intofilm.org), a Scottish education film resource.
Try to film without someone standing by to stop people walking into shot (or ruining your sound).	Have someone stand outside the door or at the end of the corridor to stop people while you are shooting.
Just point the camera, shoot and hope for the best.	Rehearse the shot.
	Let the camera run for a few seconds before and after the shot so that you can cut cleanly in the edit stage.
	Call the shots 'stand by and action for start'. Then everybody knows that you are filming.
	Ask an assistant to record the shots. Did anything go wrong? Which 'take' is the one you want to use? It will make life much easier during the credit stage.
Accept the first shot and move on.	You will probably have to do a few takes of the shot before you are happy.

Finally, don't rush this stage. You need to be very organised – even a very small production is a huge undertaking to do well.

 ONLINE

Head to the Digital Zone to learn how to make a cardboard tripod – www.brightredbooks.net/subjects

 THINGS TO DO AND THINK ABOUT

In pairs, think of a scene in a film that you know well. Re-storyboard it. You should remember to use a variety of shots and add in production notes. Think about the effect you are trying to achieve.

COURSE ASSESSMENT

ASSIGNMENT 3 – POST-PRODUCTION

POST-PRODUCTION AND DEVELOPMENT SECTION

The final steps of your production or print content often make the difference between well-finished content and something that looks a little rough or amateur. If you are working on print content take the time to cross-check your content with your plans. Look at the details closely as well as the arrangement of text and image and check you have used punctuation correctly and checked and double-checked your spelling. Ask a friend to have a quick look as well just in case you have missed anything.

The editing process in filmmaking is key to the final look of the film (see Editing, page 12). An editor has the ability to take footage and piece it together in an entirely different way altering tone and pace. You are working from a carefully thought out storyboard and plan so remember to use those notes to remind yourself of what you set out to do and why. As in the production stage there may well be parts that you want to change (and that you can do) as long as you don't create an entirely different version! Any changes that you make can be discussed in a structured way in the development section. Leave yourself plenty of time to edit; it takes longer than you think, and you have to build in time for loading clips, crashing computers and any other technical disaster that may befall you. The following are some tips to bear in mind.

DOs DON'Ts

Don't	Do
Accidently make up a new film during the editing process.	Remember your purpose and audience. Do use your plans and notes of good takes.
Delete your footage until you have finished.	Look carefully through all clips – you may just find something you want to use even if it was a discarded clip.
Use thousands of crazy transitions.	You can use continuity or non-continuity editing but transitions are tricky to do well and should only be used to enhance meaning – not just for the sake of it. In the wrong hands they look awful. Less is more.
Linger too long on a shot that doesn't do much.	Pick up the pace. Cut, add in another camera shot and cut back. There is nothing worse than a badly shot long take of something relatively unimportant. Good editing can cover up even the most dubious looking camera work.
Use dialogue that is too poor in quality to be heard.	Either fade and bring up the music track to cover the bad vocal or turn down the volume and either use a voice-over or re-record. You will be unable to synchronise raise sound with the equipment and lack of expertise that you have at this stage so be creative with sound. You should never be using dialogue unless it tells us something important about the character or moves the plot forward and so forth.
Accept your first edit.	Polish up the edit until you are really happy with the final film. Don't spoil it with sloppy credits. Check spelling. Thank everyone who helped you even indirectly – janitor, your mum, your dog and so on. They all deserve a mention as you have no money to pay them.

DEVELOPMENT SECTION

You are now ready to complete your assignment. The development section is worth 35 marks. This includes assessment of your finished content combined with an explanation of media techniques and codes that you have used. You are asked to select five examples from your content to show how you have created meaning.

You will want the strongest five examples because they will give you the most to talk about. Vary your selection so that there is no possibility of overlap or repeating yourself.

contd

Course assessment – Assignment 3 – post-production

You will only be awarded marks once no matter how many different ways you attempt to say the same thing. If you have planned carefully you will have used a variety of codes, such as layout, colour, font, camera work, lighting and sound, so there will be no need to repeat yourself.

Each section is marked out of 5 with an additional 2 marks available for the evaluation step.

The strongest answers will identify an aspect that you have used (either one specific code or throughout the whole content); describe the code clearly and accurately, and then discuss/explore both the intended/possible connotations and the impact on, for example, the target audience; preferred or differential reading or both; purpose; genre expectations; style; or anything else you want to comment on!

The structure you will use will be in response to the following questions.

> A – You will have to describe how, in your example, you have used any coded techniques and conventions. Explain why you have used them by discussing any intended connotations and meanings. (5 marks)
>
> B – You will have to evaluate both the strengths and weaknesses of the above examples. You should make reference to any big effects used or the production process itself. Include your own performance and how you would, on reflection, improve if relevant. (2 marks)

Don't worry if your content is not as professional as you had hoped; this is not the focus of the course. You are being assessed on your understanding and application of various media techniques specific to the form you have chosen. They want to see that you know how to, and have tried to, create meaning. The markers use banding to judge what each section should be awarded.

DON'T FORGET

The examiner will have your plans and content in front of them. They must all match up. The development of the idea should be evident from the brief through to evaluation and all the steps inbetween!

THINGS TO DO AND THINK ABOUT

Look at the following extract.

> A. I used lots of different camera angles in my film such as low-angle shots to reflect the main character's mood being low, and eye-line matches when I wanted the scene to be more light-hearted. The distance and relationship between the audience and the subject is important. In these shots the audience is in a position where they literally look down on the character. It makes the audience feel as if they are vulnerable and to be pitied. The eye-line matches are a contrast and this shows difference in power and confidence. The stronger characters are directly addressing the audience.
>
> B. I wish that I had used long-distance shots of my character as I feel this would show isolation as the audience would feel very distant from the subject. The shots that I have are quite intimate as they are close. Distance and isolation are key in a short film about depression. Showing them as small in a vast setting would make them look lost.
>
> I included some long shots, for example, the scene where I ignore my friends who were shouting my name. I used this to create a sense of distance between the main character and her friends and I think I did these quite well.

1. What would you award?
   - A /5
   - B /2

2. How would you have improved this?

3. If you haven't yet done this try to write your own version for one aspect of content you have made or planned. Draw a couple of frames of a scene and analyse and evaluate in detail following the instructions above.

ONLINE

Head to the Digital Zone at www.brightredbooks.net/subjects to learn more about how your paper will be marked.

COURSE ASSESSMENT

MARKING INSTRUCTIONS AND FURTHER PRACTICE

The following marking instructions are based on the General and Detailed Marking Principles for N5 Media (SQA). They have been explored further to make sure you understand the standards required.

EXPLAIN OR DESCRIBE

The two main types of questions you will be asked will ask you to either *explain* or *describe*. One question may ask you to do both.

	Question Example	How Do I Answer?	Example
Questions that Ask You to Describe	Describe in detail (from content with which you are familiar) examples of narrative codes or conventions which could be considered typical of a particular genre. 6 marks	First, check how many points you need to make in this part of the question. 1 accurate point, directly relating to the question, will be worth 1 mark. A point could be an explanation, a feature or characteristic – in this case a narrative code. You should briefly explain the code and identify the genre. Either develop your answer with an example for +1 more mark or make a new point. Continue until you have the number of marks required – in this case 6. If you are uncertain that your point is developed enough you should err on the side of caution and add a new point.	*Enigma codes keep the audience guessing* what the outcome will be and action films rely on them. 1 mark At the start of *Skyfall*, the main protagonist is shot and the audience wonder if he is really dead. (Development of that point = 1 further mark) Binary oppositions such as opposing characters are important in an action genre. Help: create conflict, add complexity and moves the story forward. (New point for 1 mark) The characters of Silva and James Bond are clear examples of this. Although they both once worked for MI6, they are now enemies. When we first meet Silva we worry that Bond may have met his match. (1 point for development)
Questions that Ask You to Explain	Explain how examples (from content that you have studied) have effectively shaped a recognisable genre. 6 marks	You must identify and *explain* relationships between the different points you have made about the key aspects. The way they work or combine to create meaning; any connotations *and, crucially, their effect*; how they appeal to audience and so on. Look for connections. (cause and effect – see below) 1 basic point = 1 mark A development of the point + 1 more mark New point = 1 mark and so on	Technical codes have been used throughout the scene where Silva is imprisoned at the new MI6 Headquarters. The scene cuts noticeably between characters as they talk, and each shot is a close-up of their reactions. (1 mark) This allows us to see subtle eye movements of the characters as they talk and react to the situation. *This in turn* (cause and effect) gives the audience understanding of how dangerous Silva actually is.

The marking instructions ask you to explain cause and effect, so it is worth looking a little more closely at this. What is cause and effect? This means that there has been a consequence as the result of a decision/action. Something is suggested or understood by a production decision, such as a camera angle, editing sequence, unusual sound or representation. Being a little more aware of the way your answers are structured will help you ensure that you address elements such as connotations, meanings and effects on audience.

Try using the following phrases in your answer to help you ensure you are considering cause and effect.

Cause and Effect Word Bank	
Therefore	… and as a result
This suggests	The effect of this is …
This therefore creates …	As a consequence …
Hence …	For this reason …

1. Try to add in your own.
2. Create some new questions – audience.

ACTIVITY: Exam practice

The following questions have been taken from SQA papers 2015–17. They have been grouped under the corresponding key aspect. You should identify which of your texts best matches each type of question. This will better prepare you for the exam as well as

contd

highlight any potential gaps! Before you tackle each question, you should create a study card for each key aspect. You can an example of a revision card at the bottom of page 79.

Key aspect: representations + institutions

Often the content maker's own beliefs and attitudes appear as specific representations in the texts they produce.

(a) Choose two representations (from content you have studied) and describe what you think each may reveal about the beliefs and attitudes of the content makers.

(b) Referring to the examples you have given in part (a) explain fully how each representation has been created (refer to key aspects such as language or narrative to help you explain each construction). marks 2 + 6

Key aspect: representation + language codes

It is likely that the representations in media content you have studied have been created through the manipulation of a variety of language codes and features.

(a) With reference to content with which you are familiar, describe two clear examples of representations you have identified.

(b) Both identify the language features used and explain in detail how each work to portray these convincing representations. marks 2 + 10

Key aspect: institution – influence of internal and external factors/controls

There are many external or internal factors that affect the production of all forms of media content.

(a) Describe two examples (from media content you have studied) of internal or external factors or controls that has had an effect on either the content or the production process.

(b) Explain how media content with which you are familiar, has been notably impacted by internal or external factors or controls. You should develop each point you make. marks 2 + 6

Key aspect: genre

Specific genres (or sub genres) will appeal to different audiences, who will in turn expect some recognisable (or obvious) conventions in order to help them make sense of the text.

(a) From media content you have studied, identify and describe examples of specific conventions of genre.

(b) Explain how several examples of the genre conventions you identified would appeal to the audience. You can use as many different texts as you need. marks 8 + 4

(a) Identify and describe two different genre conventions from a text you have studied.

(b) Explain how the conventions you picked work and how they have helped you to identify the genre. marks 2 + 6

Key aspect: narrative

In order to engage their target audience, the makers of media content often rely on the use of narrative structures, codes and conventions.

(a) From content you have studied, identify and describe two examples of narrative structures, codes and conventions.

(b) Explain how the examples you picked might work to engage the audience. marks 2 + 6

THINGS TO DO AND THINK ABOUT

Once you feel confident about answering the questions you should try them under timed conditions. Remove yourself from any distractions; time the clock for two hours and begin. This will give you a more realistic experience and better prepare you for the real thing.

ONLINE

Head to the Digital Zone and find the link to SQA past papers – www.brightredbooks.net/subjects

COURSE ASSESSMENT
FURTHER PRACTICE

QUESTIONS AND TASKS

Summary tips for exam questions

Before you try more exam questions, stop and refamiliarise yourself with the language of that question. Here is a summary to help you.

The questions will either ask you to *explain* or *describe*.

Explain – For these questions you will have to identify and explain relationships between, for example, language features and genre or representations and society.

SQA refer to this as 'cause and effect'; essentially you are making connections.

Expect 1 mark for each explanation and 1 mark for development of your point (you may have more than one development for each of your points). Continue to do this until you have done enough for the number of marks available.

Describe – Generally speaking, you will be making relevant points for 1 mark and developing with examples for a further mark/example. Continue to do this until you have done enough for the number of marks available.

Tips on answering

It is very worthwhile to make sure you are familiar with the marking instructions on the SQA website.

Make sure you can identify each new point or development point in your answer – if you can't, neither can the examiner.

Don't labour the point; you will not be given any additional points for saying the same thing in a different way. Move on.

ACTIVITY: More questions to practice

Key aspect: society

> Media content is often a reflection of society.
>
> (a) Describe in detail, aspects of the society that you have identified in texts that you have studied.
>
> (b) Explain how these aspects reflect the time that the text was made or set. You could refer to different ideologies, events or beliefs or anything else appropriate in your answer. marks 2 + 8

Key aspect: language + audience

> Media texts rely on technical and cultural codes to create meaning for their audience.
>
> (a) Describe in detail one example of a technical code and one example of a cultural code, that create meaning, from a text that you have studied.
>
> (b) Explain in detail how your chosen examples have been used effectively to create meaning. In your answer you could refer to connotations, preferred reading, differential decoding, mode of address or any other appropriate ideas. marks 2 + 8

Remember that you can use a combination of texts in your response and that your answer must be relevant to the question in order to gain marks.

contd

Course assessment – Further practice

Role of the media:

One intended function of media content is to present a public service.

(a) Describe two examples from public service content that you have studied that show understanding of a particular issue.

(b) For the examples you have given, explain how at least two key aspects have been used to achieve intended purpose. You could for example choose from genre, cultural or technical codes, representations, narrative codes, conventions or structures in your answer. marks 2 + 8

DON'T FORGET

You will not be allowed to take any notes into the exam with you. As soon as possible, practice under exam conditions.

THINGS TO DO AND THINK ABOUT

If you haven't already, now is the time to make revision cards (for help with this look at the revision section online). A good way to organise this is through each of the question types and identifying the relevant texts you have studied including key points and relationships between aspects. Use the following template and continue until you have worked through all of the potential question types (use this chapter to help you). Alternatively, you can make the focus of your cards the text.

Either way, by doing this now you will cut time nearer the exam and you will be far better off as a result.

ONLINE

Find links to SQA Past Papers at www.brightredbooks.net/subjects

Question Types	What I Can Include in My Answer	Relevant Texts	Key Points
Categories	Purpose – escapism, profit, entertainment, information Genre – action, British drama, horror, comedy, documentary Style – social realism Tone – dark, enlightening, nostalgic, revealing	Wasp Dove beauty campaign Lynx adverts Irn-Bru adverts Apocalypse Now Late Night Woman's Hour	Wasp – to entertain but not for escapism British drama Social realism Dark tone with use of humour. Tragic at points.

COURSE ASSESSMENT
PRACTICE PAPERS

PUTTING IT ALL TOGETHER

Now try the papers below under examination conditions. This means you must work under timed conditions, put away all notes and remove yourself from distractions. Remember, you will have to select a previously unseen advert for section 2 – no shortcuts!

You are allowed two hours for each paper; the papers are worth 60 marks each.

PRACTICE PAPER 1

60 marks – *Attempt all questions*

Section 1 – Analysis of media content in context
Section 2 – Analysis of a media text

Section 1 – Analysis of media content in context – 50 marks

You may refer to the same or different media texts in your response to each question.

1. Representations in media texts are created by the use of technical and cultural codes.
   a) Describe two examples of representations you have studied. 2 marks
   b) Explain in detail how technical and cultural codes have been used to construct these representations. 8 marks

2. Certain narrative codes, conventions and structures are expected in order to reinforce a particular genre.
   a) Describe two different narrative codes, conventions or structures you might expect to find in a particular genre. 2 marks
   b) Explain in detail how media content you have studied has used aspects of narrative to conform to particular genre conventions. 8 marks

3. Media content often reflects aspects of society from the time that it was made, consumed or set.
   a) Explain in detail how certain aspects of society have been reflected in content you have studied. 10 marks

4. Both internal and external controls affect the creation and content of media products.
   a) Describe internal or external controls (or both) relevant to media content you have studied. 2 marks
   b) Explain in detail how these controls have affected either the production process or final content. 8 marks

5. One role of the media is to perform a public service.
   a) Describe how content you have studied meets that need. 2marks
   b) Explain how at least two key aspects have been used to achieve this. Choose two from: language, narrative, representation, categories, institutions, audience or society. 8 marks

Section 2 – Analysis of an unseen media text

Carefully select either: an advertisement, a magazine cover or a film poster that you **have not** previously analysed. Answer the following question worth 10 marks.

Identify and explain what you believe to be the purpose of the text **and show how** the content creators have used the key aspects of media literacy to address that purpose. There may be more than one purpose. Discuss in detail who you think might be the target audience and again what key aspects the content creators have used to engage them **and how**.

You must refer to **at least two** of the key aspects (categories, language, audience, representation, institutions, narrative or society). You should ensure that you make an appropriate number of developed points for the number of marks available. 10 marks

Total 60 marks.

DON'T FORGET

If you are still struggling you can check your notes and identify what works well for each answer. It is better to address gaps in your knowledge at this point rather than when you are sitting in the exam hall.

PRACTICE PAPER 2

60 marks – *Attempt all questions*

Section 1 – Analysis of media content in context

Section 2 – Analysis of a media text

Section 1 – Analysis of media content in context – 50 marks

You may refer to the same or different media texts in your response to each question.

1 Media content relies on cultural and technical language codes to engage its audiences.
   a) Identify and describe two different language codes from media content that you have studied.   2 marks
   b) Explain in detail how each work in the context of the text, in order to engage the audience.   8 marks

2 Conventions of genre are important in making sure the text meets audience expectations.
   a) Identify and describe two different conventions of genre from content you have studied.   2 marks
   b) Explain in detail how each example has been created.   8 marks

3 Certain ideas about, or aspects of, society are both represented (and often central to) the narrative of media content.
   a) Identify two different references to aspects of society (such as ideas, beliefs or events) from content you have studied.   2 marks
   b) Explain in detail how the aspects of society have been created. You should refer to at least two key aspects in your answer.   8 marks

4 Creators of media content often use a variety of language features to create representations (for example of people, places or events). Identify and describe at least two different representations from texts you have studied and then explain in detail what aspect of language have been used to create an effective representation, **and how**. You should refer to both cultural and technical codes in your answer.   10 marks

5 Often media content performs more than one role, for example, it may entertain as well as be created to make a profit or created to entertain with a need to inform.
   a) Identify two roles of the media from media content you have studied.   2 marks.
   b) Explain in detail how each role has been established by the use of at least two key aspects. Choose two from: language, narrative, representation, categories, institutions, audience or society.   8 marks

Section 2 – Analysis of an unseen media text

Carefully select either: an advertisement, a magazine cover or a film poster that you **have not** previously analysed. Answer the following question worth 10 marks.

Identify and explain what you believe to be the purpose of the text **and how** the content creators have used the key aspects of media literacy to address that purpose. There may be more than one purpose. Discuss in detail who you think might be the target audience and again what key aspects the content creators have used to engage them **and how**.

You must refer to **at least two** of the key aspects (categories, language, audience, representation, institutions, narrative or society). You should ensure that you make an appropriate number of developed points for the number of marks available.   10 marks

Total 60 marks.

DON'T FORGET

You can try these questions again using different texts for your answers to see which work best.

ONLINE

When you have completed these papers you should head to www.brightredbooks.net/subjects for a link to the SQA N5 Media past papers. Complete all of the past papers, including the specimen paper. The more practice you get the more prepared you will be.

THINGS TO DO AND THINK ABOUT

Try to make up your own questions and swap with a friend. You can see that you can combine different questions to make new ones.

COURSE ASSESSMENT

MESSAGES FROM THE MARKERS

HELPFUL FEEDBACK

As you will be sitting an exam and submitting course work, it would be wise to consider the feedback that the media marking team provide at the end of each exam period. Some key messages have been summarised for you below and include one or two useful tips and examples to clarify.

ASSIGNMENT

Set high standards for yourself. Make sure each step of the assignment is completed to the very best of your ability. Never send in first working drafts or work done at the last minute: plan, explore, develop, review, adjust and then, only when you are happy with your submission, submit. Take pride in your work.

- Be creative – although you will be given a brief, you will have many creative decisions to make to show flair and originality.
- Standards for National 5 Media are high so be organised and be prepared to work hard.

Planning section

Planning comes *before* production – always. You are being awarded marks for your planning skills. Your markers are very experienced in recognising and differentiating between genuine planning and last-minute, panic-induced, retrospective, clutching-at-straws waffle.

- Ensure that you make sensible (and genuine) points showing cause and effect – that means the planning decisions you have made as a result of the research you have undertaken. (See the section on research on page 84 if this is something you struggle with).
- Make sure your research is thorough and relevant and always write up your research notes as you complete your research (you will never remember the details later on). It is always better to complete one part of your work fully before jumping to the next. *Never* write up your planning section after you have developed your content.
- Do be creative with your lack of resources rather than taking the opportunity to have a little rant! The results have previously shown that many candidates have excelled with very limited equipment. Be creative.

Development

- Make sure that you clearly explain, in detail and depth, the connotations and meanings created through your use of various codes.
- Always make sure your creative intentions are clear to the examiners. It's okay if your content didn't turn out as well as you had hoped but your intentions *must* be clearly explained. Markers are very clever people, but they can't mind read and will only mark what is in front of them.
- Make sure that you fully demonstrate your depth of understanding through application of your own use of media codes to create meaning or achieve a purpose. Do not repeat ideas – your response will be thin and you will not be awarded for repeated ideas.
- If you discover that you have a particular technical talent (for example, editing or camera work) make the most of this area. For example, you could evoke a sense of panic in the audience by use of a fast-editing sequence or create connotations of an unstable or vulnerable character by using a number of different camera angles, such as a Dutch tilt or a high-angle shot. Look at masters of the skill or effects you are trying to produce and try to recreate the effect (on a much smaller scale)!
- Ensure that you keep your answers detailed throughout your five response areas of the development section; do not let your answers become thin towards the end.
- To gain the 2 marks for evaluation you still have to be detailed and not repeat what you have identified and discussed in the first part of your answer. Refer back to your production log (see the section on production).

QUESTION PAPER

- First, make sure you select and match your understanding of the content you have studied carefully with each question. You may not want to use the same content for all questions. By now you should be able to discuss a full range of texts.
- Do make sure that you understand how the marks are allocated so that you can do enough for the number of marks available. (See section on question paper, page 76.)

Language

- There is no excuse for not having plenty to discuss for the type of question that asks about technical or cultural codes. It is a very open question, allowing you to discuss content of your choice: print, moving images and so on. If you are in any doubt, take a moment to revise (see chapter on language) so that you know what technical and cultural codes are – some candidates have previously discussed, for example, representation, and this will yield an incorrect answer. Before the exam you could practice a representation question and a language code question to ensure you can differentiate between them in the exam.

Narrative

- These questions are usually done well. Revise the narrative concepts that were used in content you have studied and show that you understand how it has worked in context by using detailed examples. Remember to create revision cards with key points and a sample answer to remind you of the standard required at National 5.

Representation

- Most candidates are confident when tackling representation questions and can usually explain in detail how the representations have been created (according to stereotypes or non-stereotypes, for example).
- Do remember that you can discuss representations of places and events as well as character types. As above, make sure that you have detailed notes for all of the representations that you may want to discuss in your exam on revision cards.

Genre

- Questions asking about the conventions of genre are usually done well. Always familiarise yourself with the conventions before you embark on the study or analysis of new content. This should be very straightforward if you are organised and have revised prior to the exam. Again, pick the best content for this question (for example, that which has obvious genre conventions, such as documentary, horror or adventure).

Institutional controls – internal and external

- Candidates often find this question very straightforward – especially when discussing how constraints such as regulation, censorship and any other external controls have had an effect on or influenced the final content. Do not make this up/guess – *research* and write up your notes or revision cards at the time of research. Add to them as you explore more content.

Society

- Make sure, if this question arises, that you are discussing how aspects of society have affected media content rather than how media content has affected society (this would be a role of the media question and your answer would be wrong!).

Role of the media

- Make sure that if you are discussing how the content meets the needs of the audience that you don't confuse this type of question with an audience question and discuss target audience instead. Think about separating clearly your notes on Role of the Media.

ONLINE

Head to the Digital Zone for further links, activities, tips and documents to succeed in the assessment – www.brightredbooks.net/subjects

THINGS TO DO AND THINK ABOUT

For all questions make sure you know the difference between questions that ask you to explain and questions that ask you to describe. If you see *explain* in the question: exemplify, make connection (cause and effect). This type of answer requires detail!

COURSE ASSESSMENT
HOW TO RESEARCH

Throughout your National 5 Media qualification you will have to engage in research. The following are a few tips to help you (in the context of the media course). Research is almost always independent work and the skills that you develop will serve you well beyond the school gates.

WHAT IS RESEARCH?

Research conducted in the context of your course will take a variety of different forms but will typically include watching content and making notes and reading articles, for example, from newspapers, magazines, online articles or any journals you may have access to. It may include talking to people, for example, a focus group or a target audience, in order to gauge opinions or preferences of the consumer (audience).

You may need to explore options or experiment with equipment or software until you find what works for you. The key is to try more than one option in order to see what is available and what best meets your needs. You will make discoveries and make choices – this is research as you have explored possibilities. There are many different types of editing software or desktop publishing packages available and you should look online to see what other students found worked well. If you have no experience your angle of research may be focused on the software packages that are free and easy to use for beginners (you then might download it, read the help manuals and try to do some practice work). If you are an expert, you may want to concentrate your efforts on the best free packages available that will give you the most manual control over your edit, for example.

This is all research.

You will conduct research in the traditional sense of the word; for example, your teacher may have introduced you to narrative theory, for example, the use of 'Enigmas' (see chapter on narrative). A simple Google search will inform you that Roland Barthes and his theory are key to the idea of enigmas, so you can read about the key points. This will give you a clearer understanding. Throughout the course you may want to research ideologies, use of camera angles, colour in advertising or research relating to meeting the needs of the audience theories, such as Maslow's Hierarchy of Needs.

How do I do it?

The Internet is a wonderful thing – research that would once have taken months of sourcing through journals and books is now available to you at the click of a button. The downside, however, is that even a simple search will throw up many possibilities. This can present you with too much information and it may not all be true. A search for many media topics will reveal work done by other students on media courses. The content may be very good and sometimes it may be useful by simplifying a topic *but* a word of caution – it may be inaccurate, over-simplified, give incorrect examples or omit crucial facts or information. So do have a look if you think the content may be helpful, but try to find websites that look as if they are an authority on the subject.

So, in summary – choose sites that look as if they have been written by an expert or authority on the subject. Look to see who the publishers are to make sure they are not advertising or promoting the topic or subject. For much of your research you will only be looking for a number of *key facts* to better help you understand the topic. Don't get too bogged down in complicated explanations; this will only confuse you and take up your valuable time.

Wikipedia

Remember that a Wikipedia entry can be written by anyone; that doesn't mean the posts are not helpful but do cross-check. As a beginner the BBC Bitesize may be a good bet but you could still cross-check and extend the depth of the information you require (and if you are feeling ambitious there are a number of more in-depth articles on the subject).

contd

Course assessment – How to research

How to use a search engine effectively.

A search engine is effectively a massive online library. The key to getting the results you need is to refine your search. You can use a number of different search engines; use whichever you prefer. Each search you input contains keywords that return the most popular searches with those key words. So be precise and leave out anything you do not want to appear in the results.

Use as few words as possible. Use a 'Boolean operator'. Use quotation marks if you want the search to reveal only what you have typed into the search bar and no other possibilities. Use an asterisk after the word if you wish to search all variations of it. Media*, for example, may throw up mediation as well as media.

CONTENT RESEARCH

This is perhaps the most fun of all the research strategies and about the only time you can truthfully claim that you have to watch a lot of television or film or read magazines for homework – but you do, and lots too! As a new media student, you will want to familiarise yourself to a *wide range* of content. This book has pointed you in some interesting directions and your teacher will also. A simple Google search will always dig up a wealth of other suggestions of content, style or works by the same creator or their contemporaries. You will need to look at, or watch, the original content. This can be time-consuming, but is definitely worth it – there is so much content available for free on the Internet so there is really no excuse. If you can't find the moving image content you are looking for, try researching 'key scenes' – for copyright reasons you are much more likely to find them online than the entire content.

Active research such as audience research

This is a different type of research to an online Google search but no less important. You are awarded marks for this section and you must evidence a well-planned research folio (see audience chapter p 52). The following tips will help you produce some good quality audience research.

Before you approach your target audience, decide what information you need from them – what is the purpose of your research? This is most likely to be to gauge what would attract them to your content. What would keep them interested and, furthermore, what would make them engage with the advertisement (call to action)? What would keep their interest in a short film?

Try not to be too simplistic in your answers – it is easy to say three-quarters of your audience said they liked music. How about asking them what examples they could give of similar content with music, or showing them two clips – one with and one without music, or with contrasting types of music. Which did they find more engaging? Did either example put them off watching or help reinforce the message or tone?

DON'T FORGET

This is also very useful for your English portfolio work! Duplichecker is free and does the job. A simple Google search will give you a list of others. Find one which works for you if you need to.

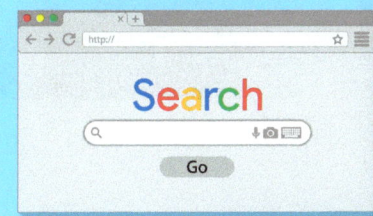

THINGS TO DO AND THINK ABOUT

Plagiarism is using someone else's words or ideas without permission. You can 'cite' authors by using quotation marks to identify their words. You are showing that you support or oppose a key idea, not copying the idea and claiming it as your own. The planning part of your assignment requires a significant amount of research, so you must be very careful not to plagiarise someone else's work. There are several good free plagiarism checkers online.

COURSE ASSESSMENT

CASE STUDY 1 – YOUTUBE AND VLOGGING

VLOGGING

A vlog is a blog containing video content. It usually involves an element of self-expression and is produced in the *form* of personal stories, or video diaries, information or tutorials. Popular examples include beauty vlogging, lifestyle vlogs or health and fitness vlogs.

Vlogging is big business and revenue is created predominantly in the form of advertising. This is because the above types of vlogs usually endorse certain products. Content is traditionally self-produced and distributed on platforms such as YouTube. When a vlogger reaches a certain number of viewers, advertisers will be keen to advertise before the content begins. The vlogger will receive payment from the advertisers – this can be very lucrative.

Although there are still rules, this type of 'author-created content' does not have the constraints and regulations of content such as film and TV.

ACTIVITY

YouTube has a number of 'Community Guidelines' and policies (such as age restrictions), which, if violated, may result in the removal of content. Research the guidelines for releasing content on YouTube.

EXAMPLE

The following is an extract from YouTube's Violent and Graphic Content policy:

> 'Increasingly, YouTube is becoming an outlet for citizen journalists, documentarians, and other users to publish accounts of what is happening in their daily lives. It is inevitable that some of these videos will contain content that is violent or graphic in nature.
>
> It's not okay to post violent or gory content that's primarily intended to be shocking, sensational, or gratuitous. If a video is particularly graphic or disturbing, it should be balanced with additional context and information. If posting graphic content in a news, documentary, scientific, or artistic context, please be mindful to provide enough information to help people understand what's going on. In some cases, content may be so violent or shocking that no amount of context will allow that content to remain on our platforms. Lastly, don't encourage others to commit specific acts of violence.'

You can see that it is more general than, for example, the BBFC guidelines, which are very detailed, clear and specific. Carefully review the BBFC guidelines and compare with the YouTube policies. There are both similarities and differences.

ACTIVITY

Consider any ways the restrictions could be problematic to someone producing content for YouTube.

Course assessment – Case study 1 – YouTube and vlogging

YOUTUBE

YouTube has provided opportunities for ordinary people to experience fame since 2005. For the very few who do succeed, the rewards are huge. This has meant that more and more content is being produced in an attempt to stand out from the crowd. The growing trend of releasing daring content in order to gain followers can push people to the extremes. On 26 June 2017, in the pursuit of fame, Pedro Ruiz created the idea for content of a stunt that went horribly wrong. Pedro instructed his girlfriend Monalisa Perez to shoot him at close range. Pedro's only protection – a hardback book. The stunt failed, Pedro was killed instantly, and his expectant girlfriend jailed. The video was never released.

With huge profits to be made for the lucky few, hundreds of thousands continue to publish content of varying genres.

The quality of much of the successful content released on YouTube now could easily rival traditional TV channels. Productions are slick and presenters professional. YouTube has come a long way since the first video of elephants in a zoo was released in June 2005.

ACTIVITY

Watch the first of 12 videos by YouTuber Benjamin Cook (NineBrassmonkeys) 'Anatomy of a YouTuber'.

The video interviews some of the most successful first-generation YouTubers such as Dean Dobbs, Jack Howard, Myles Dyer, Lex Croucher, Ed Blann, Charlie McDonnell, Tom Ridgewell, Chris Kendall, Phil Lester, Liam Dryden, Alex Day and Carrie Hope Fletcher.

This video has hundreds of thousands of views. Use the example to identify genre markers of a typical YouTube video such as direct mode of address and documentary-style content such as interviews, drama and comedy. In addition, you should closely consider the opening scene; the overall quality of production; the identification of any conventions of genre or cross-genres; tone; style; use of language codes such as camera work (movement, angles and distance); continuity or non-continuity editing; sound; music; lighting; cultural codes such as presenter/character accents; costume; representation of the three characters; and any recognisable narrative codes.

Try to identify any aspects of society that are apparent.

Finally, the video discusses the kind of people who produce, watch or engage with YouTube content. This directly relates to audience. How does this type of content meet the needs of the audience?

While working through the key aspects you should be able to draw many similarities from other content you have studied.

ONLINE

Read an article on Pedro Ruiz on www.brightredbooks.net/subjects

VIDEO LINK

Head to the Digital Zone and watch the first ever video to be published on YouTube www.brightredbooks.net/subjects

VIDEO LINK

Watch the video for this activity on the Digital Zone!

ONLINE

Head to www.brightredbooks.net/subjects for an extra activity on vlogging!

THINGS TO DO AND THINK ABOUT

Try to plan and storyboard a YouTube-style vlog of your own. If done well this could be an ideal project for you to develop for your assignment.

Start with considering purpose (to increase the amount of people following your channel, for example) and audience before deciding how you are going to create engaging content. You should storyboard your ideas just in the same way you would any other moving image. Remember to use the conventions that you have identified in the above task to help you with your ideas.

COURSE ASSESSMENT

CASE STUDY 2 – RADIO BROADCASTING

A SHORT HISTORY OF RADIO

Radio has been around since the 1920s. At that time, it was the only broadcast medium available and families used to gather with great enthusiasm around a large wireless to listen to important public service announcements and news and to be entertained by music recorded live at halls across the country. Radio took a somewhat 'secondary role' in the 1950s when TV was invented. Radio had to compete and one way that they did this was through pirate radio stations such as Radio Caroline.

Pirate radio stations were illegal as they didn't have a broadcast licence. They were famous for broadcasting the current music trend to a nation of youths. In the 1960s the British government banned all pirate radio stations, and in 1967 the BBC began to launch their own radio stations. In 1995, radio fully embraced the digital age with the introduction of DAB radio (digital audio broadcasting) and could be consumed on any number of platforms.

All radio broadcasting is regulated by Ofcom's Broadcasting Code, which both protects listeners from unsuitable content and sets standards. BBC stations operate under the Royal Charter. Commercial radio stations are privately owned and rely on advertising for revenue in the same way that independent privately owned TV channels do.

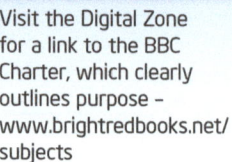

ONLINE

Visit the Digital Zone for a link to the BBC Charter, which clearly outlines purpose – www.brightredbooks.net/subjects

 **ACTIVITY**

How do you think the role of the media may differ between a commercial radio station such as West FM and a station such as BBC Radio 1?

Choose two programmes, one from each channel, and give specific examples of codes and conventions used to create purpose.

LANGUAGE CODES OF RADIO

The basic codes of radio are human voice (speech), sound effects, music and silence. They are all auditory. Radio relies on a combination of these to create meaning and communicate with the audience.

Tone

The tone of the presenter is very important and must fit in with the target audience expectations. The presenter themselves could be considered to be a language code. Accents and personalities of presenters can add the appropriate tone to a radio programme. For example, a young, Northern presenter may be more suitable to BBC Radio 1 and an older presenter with a more formal accent may be more suitable for BBC Radio 4, but it very much depends on the programme.

Sounds

Often used if listening to a play or simply an entertaining jingle! There are different types of sounds:

Action sounds (just like action props in TV) involve movement such as a plane taking off or a horse galloping.

Setting sounds set the scene in the same way that a camera would: children shouting and laughing followed by a piercing bell could indicate a school playground setting.

contd

Symbolic sounds, such as howling wind through trees and thunder and rain, may suggest an isolated and creepy setting.

Silence can also be used in a range of situations. An absence of sound can be as powerful as sound itself.

Music. Most people think of music when they consider radio. Music is incredibly powerful and has the ability to create all kinds of emotion in the listener.

Listen to a radio advertisement or a short clip of a radio programme. See how many codes you can identify and comment on.

THE BEAUTY OF RADIO AS A MEDIUM

Radio is a time-based medium rather than most other mediums that take up a physical space. Everything on radio has to be explained as there are no visual cues.

The role of the audience in radio and mode of address

Radio fuels the imagination in such a way that the audience themselves are contributing to their own reading. This is because we all imagine things differently according to our individual experiences. When a presenter is talking on the radio you feel as if they are talking to you because they are. You are the target audience and the presenter will want you to feel as if they are chatting to you in the same way that a friend might. They will often use the language of first-person direct address. It is a more intimate form of address nowadays as listeners tend to listen more on a one-to-one basis than as a family. Much radio listening, for example, happens in a car.

Radio as an institution

In comparison to TV production, it is very quick and cheap to produce radio content. Programmes can be turned around very quickly, using the same formula; you don't need such a big production crew or as much equipment. This means that live material can always be on tap for the audience.

Role of the media

1. Revisit the chapter on uses and gratifications theory. What psychological needs (of the audience) do you think radio gratifies? Give examples.
2. Find an example of a radio production and show how it meets the needs of the *creating institution* rather than the target audience.

VIDEO LINK

Go to www.brightredbooks.net/subjects and watch a short film from the highly successful campaign run by Hindustan Unilever Kan Khajura Tesan #HUL.

ONLINE

Head to the Digital Zone for more information on the 'Real Beauty' campaign – www.brightredbooks.net/subjects

ONLINE

Head to www.brightredbooks.net/subjects for an extra activity on the role of radio in underdeveloped countries.

THINGS TO DO AND THINK ABOUT

1. Marketing giant Unilever, who were responsible for the 'Real Beauty' campaign, were behind a campaign to connect rural Indian villagers by offering them a free radio station through their mobile phones. However, the radio station adverts promoted Unilever products.
    a) Watch the video and read the article on the Digital Zone. In groups, discuss whether Hindustan Unilever were benefiting the community, themselves or both.
    b) Analyse the YouTube video via the link on the Digital Zone and show how language codes or representations are used to create meaning.
2. Each BBC radio channel has a different mission statement. Why do you think this is? Try to find out what they are.

COURSE ASSESSMENT

CASE STUDY 3 – RADIO CONTENT

Lauren Laverne.

#LNWH – AN ANALYSIS

Late Night Woman's Hour hosted by Lauren Laverne is a spin-off from the established Radio 4 *Woman's Hour*. It was first broadcast on 27 October 2017. BBC Radio 4's *Woman's Hour* has been broadcasting for 70 years. Although very much a mixed-gender audience the programme offers a female perspective on current issues.

Audience demographics for Radio 4

According to BBC sources, approximately 11.5 million listeners tune in to Radio 4 each week and the gender split is approximately 49 per cent male and 51 per cent female. The age of the average listener is about 35–54 years of age. The demographic grouping is ABC1 – there is an 'upmarket bias'.

Late Night Woman's Hour is scheduled to broadcast at 11:00pm – this means that the programme is unlikely to generate a huge profit and is aimed more at a niche audience. With this in mind, you should listen to the content and consider how Laverne and the programme makers cater to their target audience.

 **ACTIVITY**

Before you listen to the programme, create a profile of the average listener. What do you think their interests are? What other media content do they consume and what sort of level of education do you think they have? What jobs or careers might they have?

The presenter

Lauren Laverne also presents BBC Radio 6 Music. From Sunderland, she has a Northern accent and is lively, intelligent and upbeat. Consider the analysis below.

Laverne introduces the topic of work–life balance and positions herself with the audience who we assume also have this problem – she starts the show by telling us that she herself has worked for 12 hours solid.

She introduces her guests (all women) as:

- Emma Gannon – writer, blogger and founder of podcast 'Control Alt Delete'
- Dr Zeena Feldman – Doctor of Digital Culture, King's College London
- Rosie Fletcher – writer, stand-up comedian, co-founder of 'Rosie and Jessica's Day of Fun' podcast and ME sufferer
- Ash Sarkar – senior editor and lecturer at Novara Media

All women appear to be successful, middle class, intelligent and career orientated.

Laverne promotes the creative projects that they are currently working on (why do you think she does this?).

Mode of address

The audience are addressed indirectly through a journalistic interview question-and-answer type style. Each guest responds in turn and they provide a range of very different answers to the questions. This ensures that audience members working in different jobs, careers or career styles are included.

Ash discusses Marxist ideologies – this is a sophisticated idea so again we can assume that the audience are educated.

> **ONLINE**
>
> Listen to an episode of the *Late Night Woman's Hour* on the Digital Zone – www.brightredbooks.net/subjects

contd

Zeena – discusses the idea that British productivity levels are way lower than in France even though we work longer hours. She suggests that we are suffering a 'death by overwork' and that in fact, on average, for every nine hours put in at the office only three are productive. 'We are working a lot, but not well.' This challenges traditional working nine to five models.

Rosie tells us she switches off by reading *Woman's Weekly* and makes reference to Victoria Wood and discusses knitting as a pass time – it's an interesting contrast to the rest of the highbrow discussion. She claims to enjoy 'traditional women's activities'.

Emma says that she needs to 'kick the addiction to social media' because the boundaries become work and rest are blurred. This is a key point in the show. In addition, she tells the audience that as she is a millennial "she doesn't need to work nine to five and did it once mostly as an experiment." Although she suggests we shouldn't all be a 'Digital Nomad' (someone who can work from anywhere earning vast amounts of money) she doesn't subscribe to the idea of traditional workplaces. This could draw in audience members in her age group.

Once again, these different perspectives may appeal to different audiences as different audiences could relate to different experiences.

Observations of society

Some very interesting points about *society* are raised throughout.

They also discuss the problem of digital technology. Key points are:

- We 'bookend' each day with technology – we check phones first thing when we wake up and last thing at night.
- We have apps for everything and rely too much on technology. 'We look to the problem to offer a solution to that problem.'
- The idea that we are always at work – working from home or homing from work – suggesting that we are dealing with home issues at work and work issues at home.
- The idea that even sleep should be high performance so that we can perform at a 'top level' during the day and that in addition we have apps for that, too.

ONLINE

You can listen to other episodes of *Woman's Hour* on the Digital Zone – www.brightredbooks.net/subjects

They discuss what they recognise as 'Emotional labour' representing the typical housewife. They discuss the Roles of Women, suggesting that they are responsible for making all the decisions such as food shopping and housekeeping. They discuss that this is an 'invisible labour' and that even if men are cooking it is often the woman that has had to buy in the food. They also explore the idea that there is actually very little (if any) down time or 'restful, restorative pursuits' for career women and that even social media is just another way for *self-promotion* and, therefore, – work!

The importance of a 'third space' or a 'restorative place' is introduced. Examples such as meditation and mindfulness were given as examples because multi-tasking really wasn't an option during such an activity. At 24.06 Rosie discusses switching off by watching 'terrible television'. She uses examples of *Doctor Who* and Netflix series *When Calls the Heart*. Remember that a differential reading may argue that she is being quite *elitist* (someone who discriminates against content that they don't think of as highbrow or superior) and that any listeners who do not think they are terrible may be less cultured than her.

These are just some observations that we could make from this media content.

ONLINE

Head to www.brightredbooks.net/subjects for an activity on podcasts.

THINGS TO DO AND THINK ABOUT

You should try to put your knowledge of this to the test – now pick your own radio episode and apply some analysis.

COURSE ASSESSMENT

CASE STUDY 4 – SOCIAL REALISM

WASP BY ANDREA ARNOLD

Social realism or socio-realism is a style of cutting-edge British drama dating back to the mid-eighteenth century. Social realism texts are usually (but not always) independent, low-budget films often attracting audiences such as arthouse, festival or TV drama. This type of TV drama or film making does not pander to an audience seeking escapism. They differ significantly from mainstream Hollywood cinema or popular culture in a number of ways. Such films aim to create a realistic and recognisable tone using a range of techniques such as:
- long, uninterrupted camera shots
- hand-held shots
- real locations
- realistic (use of profanities) and often unscripted dialogue (sometimes using non-actors)
- naturalistic lighting
- the addition of realistic sex scenes.

Society

The films usually have a social or political agenda. Social class is very important to these films. Social realism films tend to portray reality in its entirety. *Wasp* was written and directed by Andrea Arnold in 2003 starring Natalie Press and Danny Dyer.

Synopsis

Young, poverty-stricken, single mum Zoe struggles to cope with her four young children on a council estate in Dartford. We watch as she attempts to reclaim her 'pre-mum identity' and enjoy her first date in years. Unable to persuade anyone to babysit, she takes her four children with her and leaves them outside the back of a local pub to fend for themselves.

Context

Arnold herself was brought up in Dartford on a council estate as one of four children. She enjoys telling real stories about real people.

Language

Mise en scène is fundamental to portraying the themes in social realism. The setting is often dark and often making use of real locations rather than fabricated sets. *Wasp* is set on a run-down council estate in Dartford. There are very few locations allowing the audience to focus on character.

Locations

Zoe's house (kitchen and living area): dirty, basic, empty cupboards.

The streets in and around the estate: give a context as very run down in places.

On the streets outside the pub. The majority of the action takes place here. They arrive early evening and eventually day transitions into night. Arnold creates tension by cutting between these shots and those of Zoe inside the pub. The audience worry as the children wait, for hours, outside for her, hungry, bored, tired and unsupervised.

Inside the pub: a busy local pub is the backdrop for Zoe's date with an old flame 'David' (Danny Dyer). Zoe arrives without enough to buy a drink and covers up her frantic visits to check on the children as 'toilet visits'. Arnold builds tension by using jump cuts between the two locations (frequently relying on diegetic sound to jolt us out of one scene into another). This works because the audience know that the children are in danger and are expecting something bad to happen to them at any point.

Danny wants to take Zoe for a drive and as an audience we question her decisions (as she does get into the car). It is at this point that a group of drunken youths

VIDEO LINK

You can find a link to *Wasp* on the Digital Zone – www.brightredbooks.net/subjects

contd

Course assessment – Case study 4 – social realism

drop a takeaway meal onto the street. The eldest child seizes the opportunity to grab the food and feed her siblings. A wasp, attracted to the sweet sauce on the baby's face, crawls into his mouth. The children scream, blowing their cover, and Zoe runs to the rescue accompanied by a shocked David who drives them home via a takeaway food shop.

Language – technical codes

Arnold uses a hand-held camera throughout the whole film. This style of camerawork mimics the way we see in reality and is a complete contrast to a typical tripod or other Steadicam shot. At points, and especially with respect to the car park scene at the end, the camera is deliberately out of focus as it races around to keep up with the children. This makes it hard for the audience to see what is happening, which, in turn, creates a sense of imminent danger – we are sure something nasty is about to happen to Zoe's four children. The shots of the doll in the pram mirror those of her sister who is racing their baby brother in the pram as if he too were a toy.

Costume – cultural codes

Neither Zoe nor the girls wear shoes as they run through the streets of the estate at the start of the film. The children look unkempt and dirty. The baby has no nappy on, and the mother is wearing a nightdress. Later on in the film we see Zoe dressed to impress in a very short skirt, as if that is the only way David is likely to pay her any attention. She wears shoes that are too big, almost like a small child dressing up to be a 'big girl'. Zoe seems no more than a child herself at times.

Narrative structure and codes

Wasp is character-driven rather than plot-led but it does follow a simple Todorovian structure and employs a number of basic narrative codes.

- Equilibrium – We are thrown into Zoe's chaotic lifestyle as she marches herself and her children, in a state of undress, to a neighbour, who she drags from her house, with the children watching and cheering their mother on.
- Disruption – Her mundane life is disrupted on the walk back to the house by the arrival of an old flame, David, who asks her on a date. She agrees, claiming that the children belong to a friend.
- Recognition – She can't find a babysitter and has no money for food, so she makes the decision to take the children on the date and hide them. The scene of her in the kitchen counting her pennies is a good recognition point. We feel the pressures she is under. This is where we first see the wasp, perhaps symbolic that danger is never far from her.
- Repair – She tries to make up for her shortcomings by frequently promising 'treats' such as food (a packet of crisps and glass of coke to share between four), and their favourite songs on the jukebox. She tries to remain in control of the situation, but as the day darkens the mood takes on a more sinister tone. She threatens the children as she shares her fears that 'Bullet Head', the woman she attacked at the start of the film, will report her to the authorities, potentially resulting in them being 'taken away' from her.
- New Equilibrium – The date is over, her secret is out but the children are safe. We don't know if things will now improve for the family or whether David will lose interest.

Editing

Non-continuity editing is often used to disrupt the flow of the narrative. This has two functions. First, forces the audience to think a little harder about what is happening. Second, the constant jump cuts build tension; there is an ongoing sense that something bad is going to happen to the children. The sequences don't start with long shots and close in. The opening sequence starts in the midst of action as the mother takes her children with her to confront 'Bullet Head'.

ONLINE

Research other social realism British dramas. Try to watch as many as you can, looking for common traits. (You will find many clips on YouTube.) Consider other films by Andrea Arnold, Lynne Ramsay and Ken Loach. Remember that you can use your research for your assignment if you are inspired by elements of the genre.

DON'T FORGET

Enigma codes and binary oppositions create tensions. Arnold relies heavily on these codes throughout. Try to identify some examples if you can and be sure to explain the effects in detail.

THINGS TO DO AND THINK ABOUT

The significance of the wasp? What do you think the significance of the wasp is? Perhaps it acts as a reminder that if you push things too far, there will always be a sting in the tail. Danger is never far away. She lets the wasp out of her window – it soon returns.

COURSE ASSESSMENT

CASE STUDY 5 – APOCALYPSE NOW

Apocalypse Now was one of the most iconic films ever made about Vietnam. As in the final words of character Colonel Kurtz, it explores, in part, 'the horrors' of war. The film clearly exposes the moral dilemma of the US involvement in Vietnam.

An already traumatised Captain Willard is re-deployed and sent on a mission up the Nung River to capture and 'terminate with prejudice' the elusive, and now very dangerous and out of control, Colonel Kurtz. The journey upriver becomes a metaphor for Willard's own descent into darkness. *Apocalypse Now* is loosely based on the book *Heart of Darkness* by Joseph Conrad.

'MY FILM IS NOT ABOUT VIETNAM, IT IS VIETNAM'

The making of *Apocalypse Now* was one of the most notorious in filmmaking history. Filming began in the Philippines in the late 1970s and almost from day one it became apparent that they were attempting the impossible under impossible conditions but, against all odds, the film was finally finished and today is recognised as a masterpiece. Those involved in the production film were drawn into the drama and very few left the set unscathed.

Coppola's wife Eleanor recorded the making of the film in a documentary called *Hearts of Darkness*: A Filmmaker's Apocalypse.

DON'T FORGET

If you can, you should watch both the film and the documentary.

APOCALYPSE NOW FOR N5 MEDIA

The film can be analysed thoroughly and would be an excellent text to explore to answer a question on language, representation or categories.

For the purpose of this case study, we will focus on *aspects of society* represented in the text and the *institutional aspects* that impacted on the production, post-production and distribution.

Institution

1969. Saigon and traumatised Special Forces Officer Captain Benjamin Willard (Martin Sheen) is re-recruited on a covert mission in the heart of Cambodia to hunt down a renegade Colonel Kurtz (Marlon Brando) who has set up camp among a local tribe. The journey pushes Willard to the edge of insanity.

Institutional factors affecting production
- Budget. The film went way over budget. Luckily, Coppola had just finished directing the two *Godfather* films and, although it nearly bankrupted him, he invested several million dollars of his own money, re-mortgaging his house and Napa Valley Winery to finish the film.
- Casting. Coppola initially wanted Steve McQueen, Jack Nicholson, Robert Redford and Al Pacino for the main role of Willard. One by one they all refused. Finally, Harvey Keitel was cast for the lead, but it became apparent quite quickly to Coppola that he was not suitable and the unusual step was taken to fire him and replace him with Martin Sheen.
- Marlon Brando arrived on set drunk and extremely overweight. Coppola had to make a decision – first, he wanted to change the script so that his character had over-indulged in the jungle and thus his weight had increased. Brando did not agree. It also transpired that he had read neither the script nor the book and had no idea what was happening. He refused to cooperate even though Coppola spent days reading him the book. Eventually, Brando agreed to film only if he could be shot in the dark and say what he wanted.
- Ill health. Sheen was struggling with alcohol addiction, which was not helped during the making of the film as many cast and crew were regularly taking drugs as well as heavily drinking. At one point, during a particularly heavy drinking session, Sheen breaks down during filming. He can hardly stand, begins by performing some non-scripted 'tai chi' style movements before punching a glass mirror, cutting his hand badly and literally

contd

breaking down in a fit of sobs. Coppola called for a medic and tried to stop filming, but a deeply disturbed Sheen insisted he keep the cameras rolling. It was hard for the crew to witness his breakdown, but they obliged, and the scene was kept and now forms part of the opening sequence. At the time Sheen claimed to remember nothing of the incident but later admitted on camera that he remembered every second.

- Although this incident had the potential to end filming, it resulted in a sequence that could probably never have been created otherwise. Not every setback negatively affects a production.
- Sheen later suffered a heart attack on set and filming had to be delayed for months. Coppola suffered with an epileptic seizure as a result of the stress.
- Weather – the location was plagued with constant typhoons. At one point the entire set was wiped out and had to be re-built causing very lengthy delays.
- Equipment. Helicopters were used heavily in Vietnam. The US military refused to lend them any helicopters unless they changed the script. Coppola refused. The Philippine president allowed use of helicopters currently in service; however, often during a shoot they were called away to engage in a revolt in the south of the country.
- Timeline – initially estimated at six weeks, the shoot took 68 weeks. Coppola famously noted that he had never seen as many people so happy to be unemployed.

ACTIVITY

1. What effect would each of the above constraints have had on the production or the final content? Explain your thoughts.
2. There were many more constraints during the making of the film – research them now.

ONLINE

Head to the Digital Zone for some additional activities on *Apocalypse Now* – www.brightredbooks.net/subjects

DON'T FORGET

There is a difference between trivia and constraints. Most of these issues would have a knock on effect on budget.

ASPECTS OF SOCIETY AND LANGUAGE

Coppola was an experimental director and he was clear on his objectives to highlight the lack of morality during the unpopular Vietnam War. He shows this in a number of ways throughout the film.

One scene in particular where this is shown is the air attack on the Viet Cong-held village led by the brutal Lieutenant Colonel Bill 'Kilgore'.

The scene opens with the peaceful sound of children in a local school being led by a teacher to play outside. Swiftly a soldier on watch ushers them all inside. This is a stark contrast (see the narrative chapter on binary oppositions) to the scene that follows. The soldiers have been ordered to play Wagner's 'Ride of the Valkyries' on loudspeakers from the already menacing helicopters on approach – simply because it scared them even more. It is that sound that first alerts those on the ground to the impending bloody attack. We cut to a wide shot of ten low-flying helicopters on rapid approach. As the music reaches a crescendo the shot of the helicopters is intercut with those on the ground desperately running for cover. The montage picks up pace as soldiers prepare for and execute attack. Those on the ground did not stand a chance. The whole motivation for the attack appeared to be to locate and clear an ideal spot for surfing. This shows the insanity and senseless of the attacks.

In an earlier scene, Colonel Kilgore is seen to go through a pack of playing cards with the 1st Air Cavalry logo printed on the back and throw one at each dead body as a calling card, leaving the enemy in no doubt who was responsible.

'I love the smell of Napalm in the morning' – Colonel Kilgore. (Napalm – a highly flammable substance used in incendiary bombs)

ONLINE TEST

Test yourself on this topic at www.brightredbooks.net/subjects

THINGS TO DO AND THINK ABOUT

Watch the film closely and make a list of both absurd events and brutal acts. Consider what comment Coppola was making about the Vietnam War.

GLOSSARY

Anchorage – the antithesis to **polysemy** (see below). A method of tying down or fixing meaning; for example, by a shot type, or costume or style. Newspaper images, for instance, are anchored by headlines or captions and so less open to interpretation.

Auteur – French word for author. An artistic creator – usually a director – whose strong artistic style in terms of technique, voice, technical ability and personal style ensures they are considered a primary auteur (or author) of the film.

Auteur theory – Definition used to show serious work created by highly acclaimed and respected directors.

Broadsheet newspaper – refers more to style than size; traditionally larger in size they are considered more serious in tone than tabloid newspapers and have more of a focus on world news. *The Times* and *The Guardian* are two examples.

CGI – computer-generated imagery.

Connotation – metaphorical by nature. The second and deeper level of analysis. Represented by a sign (see **signifier**). If a footprint in the snow under an open window is the *denotation*, the *connotation* could be that someone has broken in.

Constraints – either external or internal influences, such as ethical and legal rules and regulations; for example, copyright and intellectual property laws that prevent your work from being stolen and redistributed. Other parameters that creators must consider could include age certification, budget, time constraints and advertising laws.

Context – the external influences that can shape a text such as social and economic influences, historical events and audience.

Continuity editing – an apparently seamless transition from one shot to another to suggest a story. Non-continuity editing draws attention to the 'cuts' for effect.

Conventions – anticipated ways in which codes are organised and included within a text. For example, recognisable in order to meet audience expectations.

Cultural codes – expectations of dress, customs, language and gestures shared and recognisable to a particular culture.

Decoding – method of extracting meaning from a text.

Demographics – classification of information – usually audience information – such as age, gender and race for use in marketing.

Denotation – the first basic level of analysis. The process of describing the literal (exact) description of what the audience can actually see or hear. See **connotation** and **signified**.

Diegetic – refers to some element within the story world, such as sound, which appears to originate from the story, that is, music that appears to be coming from a radio (diegetic sound). Non-diegetic sound is edited in afterwards, such as a sad sound to create a melancholy mood. A homodiegetic narrator is a character in the story. Examples include narrators in *The Lovely Bones* and *Apocalypse Now*. Heterodiegetic narrators are not characters in the story. Examples include news anchors, documentary voice-overs, the narrator in *The Lost Boys* and most Westerns. Autodiegetic narration is when the narrator is actually telling the story about themselves; in other words, the narrator is also the protagonist.

Discourse – the way a particular issue is framed by the media.

Encoding – the process of constructing meaning in a text by the creator.

Episode – a single production.

Film noir – a cinema that largely describes stylish Hollywood crime dramas made from 1940 to 1960. Examples include *Double Indemnity*, *The Maltese Falcon* and *Kiss Me Deadly*.

Form – the shape and structure of the content.

French New Wave – or La Nouvelle Vague – is an influential French cinematic movement of the 1950s and 1960s. Directors rejected the typical conventions of the time and were often influenced by political and social circumstances like **Italian Neorealism** but were more experimental and avant-garde (revolutionary). Major players were Andre Bazin, Jean-Luc Godard and François Truffaut (for example, *The 400 Blows*).

Gatekeepers – process where information is filtered before reaching an audience.

Generic hybridity – a combination and fusion of different elements of genre, such as information and entertainment to make infotainment.

Genre – recognisable and repeated traits that make content easy to classify. Shape the production of a text.

Hegemony – the dominance of a particular culture.

Hybrid – blending of two different types of media to create something new.

Ideology – a system of beliefs and values held by a particular group. When these ideologies are consistently presented to us, we call them dominant ideologies.

Independent film – traditionally, a production created and produced outside of a major film studio. Indi films are recognisable by their content and filmmaking style. Often low budget.

Intertextuality – a text's meaning that is influenced by another recognisable text.

Italian Neorealism – a movement of film anchored to the difficult economic and social circumstances or the era it was trying to portray. Reflection of post-war life and reality. Key directors include Roberto Rossellini, Luchino Visconti and Vittorio De Sica (*Bicycle Thieves*).

Location – anywhere filming takes place outside of the studio.

Media – the channels used to deliver communication, for example, the Internet, magazines, television, the human voice and newspapers.

Media globalisation – the emergence, domination and influence by a small number of media conglomerates (companies) on a global level.

Medium – singular form.

Mise en scène – what we see on screen. All elements such as lighting, camera, characters and set design. It is the result of a collaborative process.

Mode of address – how the text speaks to the audience.

Montage – an illusion of the compression of time created in edit at post-production. Often with intention of ramping up the energy and building atmosphere.

Non-stereotypes – do not typically conform to expectations.

Parody – a production that mocks another text.

Pastiche – a production that reproduces and celebrates some element of another, usually well-known, text.

Polysemy – the term given to show that a text is open to interpretation and has many meanings.

Psychographics – study of human traits, such as values, personalities and opinions. Useful marketing tool to ensure meeting of audience needs.

Recce – a pre-shoot visit to assess suitability for production and crew.

Satellite scenes – support kernel scenes. See the section on TV dramas for a list of functions.

Scene – at least a couple of camera shots set within a particular setting or time.

Semiotics – the science and study of signs and their meaning. Used to analyse media texts.

Series – made up of a number of episodes.

Shot – an uninterrupted series of frames.

Signified – the implied representation. Foghorn could signify danger. Fruit could signify health.

Signifier – the physical representation, that is, the sound, text or image, such as a foghorn (see **denotation**).

Signs – all the media language used in the production of a text. In print, images, text and in moving images all elements of mise en scène, cinematography, editing and sound.

Stereotypes – a simplified identification of individuals, cultures, genders and so forth based on an assumed set of 'typical' traits. Often untrue.

Story arc – the development of a storyline or character. This can go on for years in the case of an open story arc.

Symbolism – representation usually learned through our culture. The V for victory sign has come to mean peace. Many colours have come to represent different things in different cultures.

Tabloid – popular newspapers dealing with coverage of soft news stories, such as crime, disaster and scandal. Sensationalist in tone. Image heavy, less serious in style. *The Sun* and *Daily Record* are examples. Focus on national news.

Theme – such as freedom, poverty, success or isolation.

Tone – the mood of the content.

VFX – visual effects.

Voice-over – a production device where voice that is not part of the main narrative is added in post-production.